PROTECTING CHILDREN AND

Learning from Child Deaths and Serious Abuse in Scotland

PROTECTING CHILDREN AND YOUNG PEOPLE

SERIES EDITORS

ANNE STAFFORD and **SHARON VINCENT**

The University of Edinburgh / NSPCC Centre for UK-wide Learning in Child Protection

LEARNING FROM CHILD DEATHS AND SERIOUS ABUSE IN SCOTLAND

Sharon Vincent

Published by
Dunedin Academic Press Ltd
Hudson House
8 Albany Street
Edinburgh EH1 3QB
Scotland

ISBN: 978-1-903765-96-8
ISSN: 1756-0691

First published 2009, reprinted 2010 (twice)

British Library Cataloguing in Publication data
A catalogue record for this book is available from the British Library

Typeset by Makar Publishing Production, Edinburgh
Printed in the United Kingdom by CPI Antony Rowe
Printed on paper from sustainable resources

Contents

Glossary of Abbreviations

ACFRP	Arizona Child Fatality Review Program
ACPC	Area Child Protection Committee
AIM	Assessment, Intervention and Moving On Project
ASAP	Adolescent Sexual Abuser Project
CDOP	Child Death Overview Panel
CEMACH	Confidential Enquiry into Maternal and Child Health
CESDI	Confidential Enquiry into Stillbirths and Deaths in Infancy
CMR	Case Management Review
CPC	Child Protection Committee
CPO	Child Protection Order
CPU	Child Protection Unit
CSS	Child Support Service
DHSS	Department of Health and Social Security
DHSSPS	Department of Health, Social Services and Public Safety (Northern Ireland)
DoH	Department of Health
DAT	Drug Action Team
FAI	Fatal Accident Inquiry
GIRFEC	Getting it Right for Every Child
HMIC	Her Majesty's Inspectorate of Constabulary
HMIE	Her Majesty's Inspectorate of Education
LSCB	Local Safeguarding Children Board
RRT	Rapid Response Team
SCIE	Social Care Institute for Excellence
SCR	Serious Case Review
SCRO	Scottish Criminal Records Office
SIDS	Sudden Infant Death Syndrome
SSSC	Scottish Social Services Council
STRADA	Scottish Training on Drugs and Alcohol
SUDI	Sudden Unexpected Deaths in Infancy
SWIA	Social Work Inspection Agency
SWSI	Social Work Services Inspectorate
UNCRC	United Nations Convention on the Rights of the Child

Introduction

The most tragic outcome of child abuse or neglect is child death. Most children who die in Scotland die from natural causes but a small proportion of deaths are from non-natural causes and some of these deaths will be the direct result of child abuse or neglect. This book presents new information on key inquiries and reviews into child deaths or serious abuse in Scotland between 1975 and 2009. The main focus of the book is what we can learn from looking at significant abuse cases in Scotland. However, finding out about this in a Scottish context is not straightforward. There is a considerable literature around the processes for inquiring into and reviewing cases of child death and serious abuse. There is also a significant body of literature which draws together the findings from inquiries and reviews and identifies the main themes. By and large, however, the literature which is available focuses on England and Wales. Unlike the situation in England and Wales, where there have been a number of national analyses of inquiries and reviews into child deaths and serious cases, no such information is available in Scotland. Because of this, to glean insights into child deaths and significant cases in Scotland and to identify themes, learning and implications, I use a range of sources and techniques, which include setting out UK data on the number and nature of child deaths across the UK, analysing the published reports of major Scottish cases and, where useful, comparing and contrasting this analysis with published data from elsewhere in the UK.

I set the scene for the book by looking firstly in Chapter 1 at what is known about child deaths in general. Because numbers of child deaths in Scotland are small, I use data pertaining to the UK as a whole; where they can be useful, international sources are also used. It is not always easy to determine whether child abuse or neglect played a part in a child's death and the true incidence of fatal child abuse and neglect in Scotland and in the UK is unknown. There is evidence to suggest, however, that the number of child abuse deaths may be substantially under-reported in official child death statistics. Chapter 1 presents some of this evidence. It examines the main causes of child death in the UK and considers what proportion of child deaths is likely to be attributed to child abuse or neglect. Because it is difficult to determine whether a child's death has been caused by abuse and neglect, there may be more learning to be had from investigating all child deaths, rather than just those that we know to be directly attributable to these causes so the chapter concludes by considering the evidence in relation to all preventable deaths.

Chapter 2 spells out the processes and mechanisms currently operating in Scotland to review child deaths. To put this in context, the way processes operate throughout the UK are set out. Finding out what happened when a child dies is a basic human right which is now enshrined in the Human Rights Act 1998 (Rose and Barnes, 2008). There are a number of different approaches for inquiring into and reviewing child deaths in the UK and these processes are outlined in Chapter 2. In Scotland, as in other parts of the UK, there are well-established multi-agency processes for reviewing cases where children have died and abuse or neglect is suspected to have played a part in the death. These review processes have also been used more recently to investigate other cases, such as teenage deaths from suicide, or cases where children have not died, in an attempt to widen the learning. In addition, some parts of the UK have recently introduced, or plan to introduce, processes for wider review of all child deaths, in an attempt to expand child death review beyond the focus of child abuse and neglect to one of public health where the focus is on learning from all child deaths. These wider review processes are also set out in Chapter 2.

Chapters 3, 4 and 5 set out information about the key public inquiries and reviews into child deaths and significant cases in Scotland. Because the number of reports and reviews is relatively small, information from inquiries and reviews in England and Wales are referred to, to provide some comparison and check on the Scottish data. Chapter 3 identifies key public inquiries and reviews into child deaths or significant abuse in Scotland. It discusses the main circumstances surrounding the inquiries and reviews being set up, outlines the nature of the inquiries and reviews and compares and contrasts the format of the inquiry and review reports.

Prevention of child death and serious abuse requires professionals to prioritise the most serious and concerning cases but understanding what characteristics of family relationships might place children at increased risk of death or serious abuse is complex. Nevertheless, a number of studies have examined child death and significant abuse cases and produced an important body of evidence about risk factors. Chapters 4 and 5 discuss the main themes that have been identified in Scotland and elsewhere in the UK. The themes can usefully be divided into those that are connected with the child, their family and their environment and those that are connected with professional practice. Child, family and environmental themes are discussed in Chapter 4 while Chapter 5 focuses on agency themes.

The impact of inquiries and reviews on child protection policy nationally has been significant. Indeed, they have been one of the major drivers for policy and practice change in Scotland as well as in the rest of the UK. Chapter 6 tracks some of the major policy shifts associated with key inquiries and reviews at different points from 1945 to 2007. Some of the policy and practice changes introduced in response to the recommendations of inquiry and review reports have undoubtedly been positive, but questions have been raised about the extent to which policy and practice changes should be made on the back of recommendations from individual cases where things have gone wrong. Chapter 6 concludes by considering some of these reservations.

Finally, Chapter 7 pulls together some of the main themes in relation to what, we can learn from looking at cases of child deaths and serious abuse in Scotland. Learning from such cases has tended to focus on attempting to identify characteristics in children, families and environments that may be associated with increased risk of death or abuse with the aim of better predicting high risk families and preventing further incidents of death or serious abuse. This approach to learning is perhaps understandable given the history of child protection development in this country and the strong focus within policy and practice on identifying risk.

> The crucial role for the researcher thus becomes one of establishing the characteristics associated with actual or potential abuse, while the role of the practitioners is concerned with learning these facts or indicators so that they can then identify cases of actual or potential abuse. (Parton, 1996, p. 47)

There is now a strong body of evidence about child, family and environmental factors which may be associated with abuse and neglect and much of this evidence is presented in this book alongside new evidence drawn from cases in Scotland. While practitioners should be aware of this evidence and use it to inform their practice it is, however, important to remember that we actually know very little about the causal pathways to abuse and neglect. How the various factors which have been identified interact and result in serious abuse and neglect is extremely complex and we are still unable to predict with any certainty where serious abuse or neglect is likely to occur. For this reason the extent to which inquiries and reviews into child deaths and serious abuse are seen as a useful vehicle for generating lessons to be learned has been questioned. Evidence from other countries that is presented in this book suggests that a public health approach which focuses on preventing all deaths, rather than just those that are known to be the result of abuse and neglect, might be a more effective way of learning.

CHAPTER 1

The nature and extent of child death and serious abuse

Introduction

This chapter examines the main causes of child death in the UK and considers what proportion of these deaths is likely to be attributable to abuse and neglect. It is not always easy to determine whether child abuse or neglect played a part in a child's death and there is evidence to suggest that there may be substantial under-reporting of deaths from abuse and neglect. There may be more to be learned from considering all child deaths and determining which ones may have been preventable than from focusing on deaths that are known to have been caused by abuse and neglect. The chapter, therefore, concludes by looking at preventable child deaths. Because of the small numbers involved it is difficult to obtain Scottish data on non-natural child deaths. Most of the data presented in this chapter are, therefore, UK data or data from England and Wales, where numbers are higher and more reliable. Processes for reviewing all child deaths have only recently been introduced in the UK (see Chapter 2 for an outline of these new processes) so the evidence in the final section of the chapter on preventable child deaths relies predominantly on data from outside the UK.

NUMBERS OF CHILD DEATHS

Child deaths in the UK

- Each year around 5,000 children under 15 die in the UK.
- A further 1,000 young people die between the ages of 15 and 19.
- Mortality risks are highest in infancy (around three-quarters are under one), and there is a second rise in adolescence.
- Mortality is higher in boys than girls at all ages. (Office for National Statistics, 2007)

The Confidential Enquiry into Maternal and Child Health (CEMACH) child death review study (Pearson, 2008) is the largest study to date of child deaths in the UK. It provides an overview of all deaths in children and young people aged 28 days to 18 years that occurred between 1 January and 31 December 2006 in the South West, West Midlands, and North East of England and in Wales and Northern Ireland. There were 957 such deaths in these areas over this time frame. The study covered a third of the UK child population but Scotland and large parts of England, including the whole of the South East, were excluded.

The CEMACH child death review study only included child deaths from 28 days because CEMACH has a separate national core dataset and surveillance programme on neonatal deaths (those that occur in babies less than 28 days of age). In the five regions covered by the CEMACH child death review study there were 732 neonatal deaths during 2006, representing just over two-fifths of all child deaths in these areas in 2006 (CEMACH, 2008). Most of these deaths were of babies who never left hospital but there were some unexpected deaths in the community of babies under 28 days.

The CEMACH child death review study detected child deaths at the rate of 2.47 per 10,000 children (Pearson, 2008). Of the 957 children over 28 days old who died, 512 were boys, 431 were girls (in 14 cases gender was not known). There was little discrepancy between boys and girls in the younger age groups but there was a clear tendency for higher numbers of deaths in boys than girls among school-age children and adolescents. Mortality rates for children of Pakistani and Black African origin were significantly in excess of the rate seen in white children. Death was also more common among the more socially or economically deprived, which may explain some of the ethnic differences. There were regional differences in the mortality rates of older children with the highest rates found in the North East and Northern Ireland. Again deprivation may explain some of these differences.

CAUSES OF CHILD DEATH

Official statistics compiled from information on death certificates provide an overview of the incidence and causes of child death but are limited in their ability to provide in-depth information about the circumstances which contributed to such deaths (Bunting and Reid, 2005). Research examining data on 295 infant deaths, and deaths of pre-school children referred to coroner's services across England, noted that records generally contained very little information other than the causes of death, age and sex of the child (Creighton, 2001).

Most deaths in childhood are due to natural and organic causes and are the expected consequence of natural disease processes. Some natural deaths are, however, unexpected. The main causes of death vary throughout childhood reflecting different risks and different developmental stages:

- most neonatal deaths are related to congenital malformations, prematurity and low birth weight or complications of pregnancy, labour or delivery;
- during later infancy, congenital malformations and perinatal conditions remain important causes, alongside infections and other medical conditions; a quarter of infant deaths are due to Sudden Infant Death Syndrome (SIDS) and various external causes;
- during the middle childhood years natural causes of death predominate, with infections, cancers and other medical causes accounting for 80% of deaths;
- during the adolescent years (15 to 19) the pattern is strikingly different: half of deaths are from external causes, including accidental deaths, homicide and suicide (Office for National Statistics, 2007).

Overall, unexpected deaths, including those due to a previously unrecognised identifiable cause and those that remain unexplained, together with both accidental and non-accidental trauma, account for between 30 and 50% of all childhood deaths (Office for National Statistics, 2007).

Natural causes accounted for the majority of child deaths in the CEMACH child death review study (Pearson, 2008): 77% of all deaths occurred in individuals with previous history of a medical condition or some sort of developmental delay, impairment or disability. Almost three quarters (73%) of these deaths from natural causes occurred in hospital, 19% occurred at home and 2.6% in hospices. Infection was relevant in a fifth of natural deaths overall, the greatest number being in the one to four age group.

The CEMACH study identified 229 non-natural deaths, the dominant category being deaths from road traffic accidents. Cases of death due to non-natural causes are relatively rare when road traffic accidents are excluded. Boys outnumbered girls in road traffic accident deaths, particularly in the older age groups.

The CEMACH study detected higher rates of suicide than previously reported. Suicide was the largest single category of non-natural deaths after road traffic accidents. Boys accounted for much higher proportions than girls for deaths by suicide (of the 26 suicide cases 19 were boys, seven were girls); there was a significantly higher rate of child suicide in Northern Ireland. All the children who died as a result of suicide were 12 or over; six (five boys and one girl) were under 15.

Twenty-two children died as a result of drowning and analysis of these deaths revealed a substantial effect by age and gender: this cause of death was dominated by older children, who drowned in a wide variety of circumstances including marine or boating incidents and boys accounted for much higher proportions of deaths by drowning than girls. There were low numbers of deaths from falls (18), fire or burns (12), homicide (12) and substance misuse (eight). Boys accounted for much higher proportions than girls for deaths by homicide and substance misuse.

A hundred non-natural deaths in the CEMACH study were classified as SUDI (sudden unexpected deaths in infancy). SUDI accounted for 10% of total deaths. A quarter of SUDI deaths were in babies born at less than 37 weeks, or weighing less than 2500g.

DEATHS FROM CHILD ABUSE AND NEGLECT

It is not always easy to determine whether death is due to child abuse or neglect and the true incidence of fatal child abuse and neglect is unknown. The World Health Organisation's international classification of diseases coding system, which is used to define the cause of death on death certificates, significantly under-ascertains the number of child fatalities caused by child maltreatment. The World Health Organisation estimates that 155,000 deaths in children younger than 15 occur worldwide every year as a result of abuse or neglect but only a third of these deaths are actually classified as homicide (cited in Gilbert *et al.*, 2009).

Homicide comprises murder, manslaughter and infanticide (the killing of an infant aged less than 12 months by a mother whose mind is disturbed from the effects of childbirth or lactation). There are fewer than 10 recorded cases of infanticide a year (Wilczynski, 1995). Child homicide was rare in the CEMACH child death review study (Pearson, 2008). Although numbers were very small (there were just 12 cases), there were ethnic differences. Five out of 12 cases occurred in non-white ethnic groups, which is disproportionate to the overall ethnic distribution of the deaths.

Research that reviewed files from the Director of Public Prosecutions estimated that the incidence of fatal child abuse in England and Wales may be double that of official homicide figures (Wilczynski, 1995). Some cases of homicide will be covert and hard to identify because it may be difficult to determine whether the death was intentional or not. It is estimated that there may be 30 to 40 infant deaths from covert homicide each year in England and

Wales (or unrecognised fatal child abuse or deaths arising from unrecognised maltreatment), representing about 10% of the current annual total of SUDI.

If we want to accurately assess the number of fatal child abuse and neglect cases we need to look beyond homicide rates. Pritchard and Sharples (2008) used World Health Organisation data to compare children's 'violent' deaths in England and Wales with those in other major developed countries between 1974 and 1976 and 2000 and 2002, in an attempt to explore how effective England and Wales have been in protecting children compared to other major developed countries. To account for possible 'hidden' under-reported abuse deaths they also analysed undetermined 'other external causes of death' and fatal accidents and adverse events, as well as homicides. They found that 'violence related' deaths of children of all ages had declined in England and Wales and concluded that this decline was possibly representative of steady progress in protecting children from the extremes of abuse.

The most accurate incidence of deaths from abuse and neglect have been obtained from countries where multi-agency death review teams have analysed the causes of child fatalities, such as the US and Australia (Jenny and Isaac, 2006). Analysis by child death review teams has provided evidence that child abuse deaths may sometimes be misdiagnosed on death certificates. In their analysis of the deaths of children under 18 between 1995 and 1999 using data from the Arizona Child Fatality Review Program (ACFRP) Rimsza *et al.* (2002) determined that five out of 67 child abuse deaths were misdiagnosed as attributable to natural or accidental causes on the death certificate. In three of these five cases the child was in a persistent vegetative state and died many years after the episode of abuse.

To accurately assess the number of child deaths from abuse and neglect in the UK Levene and Bacon (2004) argue that we need to pool data from a large population and undertake a comprehensive investigation of every SUDI, which includes a thorough assessment of a child's history as well as a detailed post-mortem examination. A study of sudden unexpected deaths in infancy was carried out in five English health regions as part of the Confidential Enquiry into Stillbirths and Deaths in Infancy (CESDI) from 1993 to 1996 (Fleming *et al.*, 2000). The study included all post-perinatal sudden unexpected deaths from a population of nearly 13 million. Twenty-two deaths were not studied in detail because they were subject to police investigation but the authors point out that all or most of these deaths would have ended up in the official homicide figures anyway. The remaining 417 deaths (of which 346 were attributed to SIDS and 71 to a specific cause), were subject to a case control study and to confidential inquiry. After scrutiny of personal and family histories, full circumstances of each death and reports of extensive post-mortem examination, expert panels concluded that maltreatment was the main cause of death in 6.4% of cases categorised as SIDS and in 6% of cases for which a specific cause had been attributed. Maltreatment was cited as a secondary or alternative cause of death in 8.1% and 5.6% of cases respectively. Maltreatment was defined widely and encompassed a range from deliberate smothering to negligence and poor care. On the crude assumption that all the cases attributed primarily to maltreatment and half the cases attributed secondarily or alternatively to maltreatment resulted from covert homicide, the authors concluded that the proportion of covert homicides among SIDS at that time would be around 10% (Levene and Bacon, 2004).

Analysis of 37 unexpected infant deaths in Leeds (Hobbs *et al.*, 1995), by health and social services professionals, also highlighted how gathering information from a wide range of sources can make a valuable contribution towards elucidating the cause of death. Prior to the review these 37 cases had all received a post-mortem and the cause of death had been listed as SIDS (28), SIDS plus major infection (4), bacterial meningitis (2), heart disease (2) and drowning (1). Following detailed collection of information from the family, health services and social services, issues concerning abuse and neglect were revealed in 27 of these cases and in 10 of these cases abuse and neglect were classified as a major concern.

Sidebotham's (2007) recent analysis of unexpected infant deaths has been particularly helpful in terms of categorising child deaths from abuse or neglect. Sidebotham distinguished five categories of maltreatment-related deaths:

- infanticide and 'covert' homicide;
- severe physical assaults;
- extreme neglect/deprivational abuse;
- deliberate/overt homicides;
- deaths related to but not directly caused by maltreatment, including suicides and deliberate self harm.

Brandon *et al.* (2009) used this classification to analyse cases of child deaths in the most recent biennial analysis of Serious Case Reviews in England. They found that severe physical assaults, cases of extreme neglect and covert homicides were most concentrated in infants and children under five whereas overt homicides were more evenly distributed by age; suicides and deaths from deliberate self harm occurred from age eight upwards.

PREVENTABLE CHILD DEATHS

Inherent in the definition of child death review is the concept that a large number of child deaths may have been preventable. If the number of deaths from abuse and neglect is underestimated on death certificates then we may learn more about these deaths and how to prevent them if we review child deaths more widely and do not focus solely on deaths from abuse and neglect.

Immunisation, antibiotics and improved living standards have done much to reduce levels of child mortality in the UK, as in other industrialised countries. A study by Moore (2005) demonstrates the considerable advances that have been made within the last two decades. Comparing current mortality rates of children under five in Wolverhampton with rates found in a study 20 years before, Moore found that far fewer children now died from birth injuries, accidents and treatable conditions; the number and proportion of sudden unexpected deaths also fell considerably between the two studies. In the 2005 study seven deaths were the result of deliberate harm. There were no deaths from abuse in the earlier study but Moore points out that some of the deaths which were registered as SIDS may actually have been the result of smothering.

Research in both the US and the UK suggests that significant proportions of deaths may be preventable. Rimsza et al. (2002) analysed the deaths of children under 18 between 1995 and 1999 using data from the Arizona Child Fatality Review program. A child's death was defined as preventable if an individual, or community, could reasonably have done something that would have changed the circumstances that led to the death. Arizona's child death rate was above the national average and the study found that 29% of deaths (1416 out of 4806) could have been prevented. Their conclusions were as follows.

1. Preventability increased with the age of the child: only 5% of neonatal deaths were considered preventable but 38% of deaths in children older than 28 days were considered preventable and by age nine 56% of deaths were considered preventable.
2. Deaths attributable to medical conditions were far less likely to be considered preventable than deaths attributable to unintentional injuries: 8% of deaths attributable to medical conditions were considered preventable compared to 91% of deaths attributable to unintentional injuries.
3. A few deaths due to medical conditions were considered preventable due to inadequate emergency medical services, poor continuity of

care and delay in seeking care because of lack of health insurance, and four deaths resulting from infections were vaccine preventable.

4. Nine per cent of deaths attributable to sudden infant death syndrome were considered preventable. These deaths were attributable to unsafe sleeping arrangements resulting in unintentional suffocation.

5. Almost two thirds (61%) of child abuse deaths were considered to be preventable. Interestingly much of the responsibility for preventing child abuse deaths was deemed to rest not with professionals but with community members (relatives, neighbours etc.) who had been aware of the abuse but failed to report it.

6. Many of the deaths from motor vehicle crashes were considered preventable in that children were unrestrained or inappropriately restrained and some of the deaths from drowning could have been prevented if pool fencing had been in place.

In Philadelphia more than a third (37.2%) of 607 deaths of children and youths under 21 reviewed in 1995 were considered preventable (Onwuachi-Saunders *et al.*, 1999). In the case of injury deaths 95% (224) were judged to be preventable. Twenty-nine preventable fire/burn injury deaths were associated with lack of a smoke detector, non-supervision of children and faulty home appliances.

In the UK, multi-disciplinary panel review of 126 cases in the CEMACH study (Pearson, 2008) identified factors which might have helped prevent death in 31 cases. These factors could not be detected from the dataset which CEMACH collected on all deaths, nor were they discernible from entries on death certificates. The panels encountered instances where parents' or carers' negligent behaviour may have contributed to the death as well as instances where professional practice may have been a contributory factor.

- There were examples of health care practitioners failing to recognise serious illness in children.

- There were examples of failure to take sufficient care with history or examination, inadequate observation, failure to anticipate or recognise complications or follow published guidance.

- There were situations where children who failed to attend primary care or mental health appointments were not followed up (failure to follow up was sometimes the result of health trust policy which unfairly disadvantaged the child).

- The majority of children who died following suicide or substance abuse were not in contact with mental health services and death might have been prevented if they had been.

- There were example of deaths that could have been prevented if a vaccine had been given on time and following specialist advice.

- A critical lapse in parental supervision was a recurrent feature in accidental and traumatic child death in the younger age groups, including failure to supervise the child adequately; dangerous sleeping arrangements such as co-sleeping in cases of SUDI; being the source of access to drugs involved in the child's death; taking drugs or alcohol while responsible for looking after children; poor decision making; delay in recognising that children were ill; driving badly; and smoking.

- There were examples of deaths due to children not being provided with safety belts; lack of fencing around pools; unprotected machinery or mechanical apparatus; misuse of in vehicle restraints; failure to wear safety clothing, e.g. life jackets and cycle helmets; and absence of fire alarms.

The CEMACH study concluded that timely immunisation, accurate diagnosis of acute illness, continuity of care and regular review of children with chronic disease, availability of palliative care and recognition of at risk teenagers by professionals would result in safer care of children. Recommendations included that GPs should be alert to children who re-present on three or more occasions during the course of an evolving illness; the medical concept of an 'at risk' child should be extended to all children with chronic disease; children with epilepsy should have at minimum an annual review; and children with an exacerbation of asthma should be reviewed within a few days of starting a short course of oral steroids to assess response to treatment. Many aspects of failure of care and poor decision making that were identified, for example, no bicycle helmet or seat belt, could potentially constitute neglect. The study concluded that this needed to be tackled at an individual as well as societal or governmental level. It recommended that the local authority should work with health visitors, school nurses and teachers to provide safeguarding education at an individual as well as community level, for example, in respect of co-sleeping and smoking in SUDI.

CONCLUSION

This chapter examined the main causes of child death in the UK, considered what proportion of deaths is likely to be attributable to abuse and neglect and considered the extent to which child deaths might be preventable. It found that:

- ❏ each year around 5,000 children under the age of 15 die in the UK;
- ❏ mortality risks in the UK are highest in the youngest age groups, with a second rise in adolescence;
- ❏ unexpected deaths account for between 30% and 50% of all childhood deaths in the UK;
- ❏ around three-quarters of all child deaths in the UK are from natural causes;
- ❏ deaths due to non-natural causes in the UK are relatively rare when road traffic accidents are excluded;
- ❏ the true incidence of fatal child abuse and neglect in the UK is unknown but numbers are likely to be higher than those recorded in official statistics;
- ❏ research in the US and UK suggests that significant proportions of child deaths may be preventable.

Chapter 2 outlines the processes and mechanisms currently operating in Scotland and other parts of the UK to review child deaths and significant abuse cases.

Processes for inquiring into and reviewing child deaths and serious cases

Introduction

Finding out what happened when a child dies and a public authority may have been involved is a basic human right now enshrined in the Human Rights Act 1998 (Rose and Barnes, 2008) and all parts of the UK have developed processes for inquiring into or reviewing child deaths. In exceptional cases a public inquiry may be commissioned by government but most inquiries or reviews are commissioned at a local level. All parts of the UK now have well-developed processes for reviewing deaths and serious injury where abuse or neglect is a known factor or suspected. In addition to processes for reviewing deaths from child abuse and neglect some parts of the UK have recently introduced, or plan to introduce, processes for wider review of child deaths in an attempt to expand child death review beyond the focus of child abuse and neglect to one of public health. This chapter outlines the processes and mechanisms currently operating in Scotland to review child deaths and significant cases. To put this in context, the way processes operate throughout the UK are also set out.

PUBLIC INQUIRIES

Processes of inquiry and review

INQUIRIES

- Statutory inquiries ordered by governments
- Inquiries commissioned at local level by a health or local authority, Local Safeguarding Children Board (LSCB) or Child Protection Committee (CPC) and carried out by an independent panel of investigators which may or may not have an independent author of the overview report
- Inquiries carried out internally by health or local authorities

REVIEWS

- Reviews commissioned at local level by a health or local authority, Local Safeguarding Children Board or Child Protection Committee and carried out by an independent panel of investigators
- Management reviews undertaken internally by public agencies

Under the Inquiries Act 2005 any public body or government department in the UK may initiate an inquiry into issues which it considers to be of public concern. There are different types of inquiry with different legal powers and processes. Inquiries do not normally have a remit to examine the conduct of criminal investigations held in relation to a case. Rather their purpose is to examine the role of agencies who were involved in the case up to the point at which the death or serious abuse took place, to establish whether any lessons can be learned and to make recommendations to improve practice.

There appears to be little rationale behind the process of selecting cases to proceed to an inquiry. It is often difficult to ascertain how a particular style of inquiry is determined for any particular case or how the decision was made to conduct an inquiry at all. Local issues sometimes determine whether the death or injury of a child results in a formal inquiry. In other cases inquiries may be instigated by media exposure. The media has played a key role in magnifying the profile of some inquiries. Other inquiries have come about as a result of pressure from a range of sources, including families and local communities. Formal inquiries are sometimes undertaken because a more informal inquiry has already been carried out but has failed to satisfy all the parties involved (Reder and Duncan, 2004; Corby, 2003; Corby et al., 2001; Stanley and Manthorpe, 2004).

Prior to 1975 most inquiries into child deaths were set up by the Secretary of State for Social Services. Since the Children Act 1975 all public inquiries into child deaths or other serious cases of abuse ordered by central government have been statutory inquiries. There were public inquiries into child deaths and serious abuse cases before 1975 but these were not statutory inquiries. Statutory inquiries are normally conducted in public but parts of the inquiry may be held in private. They are usually held in a quasi-judicial way and are often chaired by lawyers. They have powers that other types of inquiry do not – they can compel witnesses, enforce the production of documents and pay legal and other costs to witnesses. Professionals are often not named in reports and are, therefore, given some degree of protection (Corby et al., 2001; Hallett, 1989).

Until the 1990s most public inquiries in the UK were concerned with the deaths of children who had been physically abused while living with parents or carers in the community. In contrast, in the 1990s concern shifted to the abuse of children in residential homes and schools. Knowledge of maltreatment, particularly sexual abuse, was broadening. Reports came forward of children in residential care who had been abused in the past or were currently being abused, and inquiries were held into the practice of individual institutions or individual staff rather than into cases of abuse of individual children. Only four out of 50 inquiries in the UK from 1945 to 1990 concerned residential care whereas from the 1990s inquiries into residential abuse took place in roughly equal numbers to those into abuse at home (Corby *et al.*, 2001; Corby, 2003).

Public inquiries commissioned by governments are rare in the UK. They figured most prominently in England and Wales in the 1970s and early 1980s and have generally been replaced by less formal types of inquiry.

CASE REVIEW PROCESSES

Inquiries or reviews commissioned by local authorities and health authorities are most often used to investigate child deaths and significant abuse cases in the UK. Such inquiries or reviews do not have the power to compel witnesses or produce documents but some have been undertaken in the same adversarial manner as a statutory inquiry and may result in a publicly available report (Corby *et al.*, 2001).

All parts of the UK have processes for reviewing serious cases. Case review processes vary in different parts of the UK but have the same overall purpose – to establish whether lessons can be learned from a case in terms of improving inter-agency working and better protecting children. Case review is intended to be used as a learning tool, not as a means of attributing blame.

Serious Case Reviews (SCRs) in England and Wales

England and Wales were the first areas of the UK to introduce guidance on local serious case review processes in 1988 (DoH/Welsh Office, 1988; Department of Health, 1991b). The introduction of local serious case review processes was a deliberate move away from the type of large-scale, inquisitorial-style inquiries that characterised the 1980s. The guidelines introduced a new process by which Area Child Protection Committees (ACPCs) would undertake case reviews, known as Part 8 Reviews (Rose and Barnes, 2008), in cases where children had been fatally abused, or abused with serious physical and psychological consequences. Local authorities informed the Department of Health of every case that was subject to a case review and could make their reports public if they considered there was sufficient public concern about the case. In exceptional cases the government still ordered a public inquiry (Corby *et al.*, 2001; Sinclair and Bullock, 2002; Corby, 2003). The guidelines for conducting case reviews were revised in England in the 1991 and 1999 versions of Working Together to Safeguard Children when the term 'Serious Case Review' was first introduced and in 2000 in Wales when the National Assembly produced its own version of Working Together to Protect Children for Wales.

The Children Act 2004 and its accompanying regulations placed SCRs on a statutory footing in England and Wales. It is now mandatory for Local Safeguarding Children Boards (LSCBs), which replaced ACPCs, to conduct an SCR if a child dies and abuse or neglect is suspected to be a factor in the death. Whereas ACPCs were responsible for conducting a case review SCR has now become a *statutory function* of LSCBs (Brandon *et al.*, 2008; Rose and Barnes, 2008). The basic framework for the conduct of reviews is the same as it was before 2004 but the criteria for determining when an SCR should be undertaken are now broader, including the death of a parent through domestic violence, the death of a child at the hands of a parent with a mental illness and a child's death through suicide. Until 2004 SCRs typically focused on deaths from severe physical assault or extreme neglect but there is evidence to suggest that more recently a broader approach has been taken to include suicide, deaths related to domestic violence incidents and other deaths related to but not directly caused by maltreatment, suggesting that LSCBs are taking the new criteria seriously (Brandon *et al.*, 2008; Rose and Barnes, 2008).

Since 2007 Ofsted has had for the first time responsibility for evaluating the quality of SCRs against a set of grade descriptors and in accordance with an evaluation template. Ofsted assesses the extent to which the review fulfilled its purpose by reviewing the involvement of agencies, the rigour of analysis and the capacity for ensuring that the lessons identified are learned. Reports are graded as 'outstanding', 'good', 'adequate' or 'inadequate'. Owen (2009) has criticised the fact that Ofsted's emphasis is on the quality of the report:

> No attention, however, is being paid to what makes a good quality serious cases review *process*. There is nothing in the grade descriptors used by Ofsted that would indicate any thinking has been done about either the methods by which a serious case review should be carried out, or the areas of academic research and discussion which might be relevant. (p. 267)

As a result of growing criticism the quality assurance role of Ofsted is being defined more widely than the overview report itself. Since 2004 an independent author for the SCR overview report has been a requirement. Interestingly, however, Ofsted (2008a) found there was no correlation between the quality of the overview report and the independence of its author, a finding also in the Rose and Barnes study of 2008.

Sinclair and Bullock (2002) were critical of the fact that families were excluded from the SCR process. The latest edition of *Working Together* (HM Government, 2006) addressed their criticisms by requiring agencies to consider not just whether, but how, family members should be involved. New Welsh Guidance published in the same year (Welsh Assembly Government, 2006) also stated that the review panel should consider how family members could contribute to the review and who should be responsible for facilitating their involvement. Rose and Barnes (2008) found that family members had contributed in a fifth of the SCRs they analysed that were completed in the period 2003–5. They stated, however, that this may not have been the full picture since family members may have declined an invitation to contribute, the circumstances of the case may have made it inappropriate for them to contribute, or the report may not have recorded discussions or negotiations about family involvement. Families were involved in nine out of 47 of the cases Brandon *et al.* (2008) studied in depth in the period 2003–5. In a small number of cases the child also contributed. Ofsted (2008a) commented that it was not clear how much effort went into seeking families' participation but they found little evidence that agencies were working with families when undertaking SCRs:

- 8 out of 50 of the case reviews they evaluated recorded that families made a contribution;
- a further 8 noted that families were invited to contribute but declined;
- in 19 case reviews the issue was not covered at all;
- in 11 there was a statement that family members were not involved;
- a positive decision not to involve family members was noted in 3 reviews.

Rose and Barnes (2008) comment that the requirement to involve family members is a major development which requires appropriate facilitation, planning and resources. They stress that family members' expectations about the process should be considered since they may expect the SCR to be more like a public inquiry. Involvement of family members also raises issues about what they are prepared to have recorded and considered as part of the review since they may understandably be reluctant to contribute information that could cast themselves or other family members in a negative light.

Both the English and the Welsh guidance (HM Government, 2006; Welsh Assembly Government, 2006) include some guidelines on the format of the review report. Rose and Barnes (2008) found, however, that reports in England varied in length, style and presentation:

- half the reports they analysed were under 30 pages long but a fifth were more than 75 pages;

- there was variation in the use of genograms and some reports omitted a genogram altogether;

- a quarter of reports highlighted lessons for national policy and practice as well as local lessons;

- recommendations were generally relatively few in number (up to 20), focused, specific and capable of implementation, but in 12 reviews there were up to 40 recommendations, one review had 40 to 60 recommendations, and one had 80.

The English guidance states that reviews should be completed within four months of the LSCB chair's decision to initiate a review and the Welsh guidance states that a review should normally be completed within six months. Twelve per cent of the reviews analysed by Rose and Barnes (2008) in England were completed within the timescales laid down, or nearly so, and a further third completed within 12 months of the incident. Approaching half (45%) took over a year to complete and 17% of reports were not dated. Ofsted (2008a) judged a large proportion of case reviews as inadequate because of the time it took to complete them. It was not uncommon for SCRs to take more than a year to complete and some took as long as three years.

The Department for Education and Skills review of LSCBs (2006) found there was substantial variation in the way LSBCs in England handled SCRs. They were not always confident about their capacity to conduct reviews which were very resource-intensive. In some cases reviews were only undertaken after a long delay and some took a long time to complete. The Third Joint Chief Inspectors' Report into safeguarding children in England (Ofsted, 2008b) also pointed to serious delays in the production of SCRs in most cases. Local variations in the number of SCRs were not fully explained by the number of deaths in each area. The report concluded that LSCBs were interpreting the guidance inconsistently and some were not giving priority to SCRs.

A Welsh review (*Local Safeguarding Children Boards, Wales: Review of Regulations and Guidance 2008*) found that the costs of undertaking SCRs were an increasing burden on LSCBs. The review team acknowledged that it was difficult for LSCBs to factor in such costs since they varied according to the complexity of the case and, in some cases, the need to appoint an independent person to prepare the overview report.

There have been attempts to learn from SCRs at national as well as local level through collation of findings in England and Wales. In the 1990s several studies collated and analysed data from SCRs in England (James, 1994; Falkov, 1996; Reder *et al.*, 1993; Reder and Duncan, 1999). A government commitment was made in 1999 to national biennial analysis to ensure a continuous stream of data collection and analysis enabling an accumulation over time. The first of these biennial reviews, by Sinclair and Bullock, was published in 2002; two further reviews by Rose and Barnes and Brandon *et al.* were published in 2008 and a fourth review by Brandon *et al.* was published in 2009. In addition the Secretary of State for Children, Schools and Families announced in October 2008 that the government would carry out a study to examine the processes of commissioning, conducting and implementing SCRs. This study will report in summer 2009.

In Wales studies of SCRs have also been commissioned to inform policy (Owers *et al.*, 1999; Brandon *et al.*, 2002; Morris *et al.*, 2007). Depending upon the number of SCRs they receive, the Welsh Assembly Government has undertaken to commission overview reports every two years to draw out key findings and consider their implications for policy and practice.

Case Management Review in Northern Ireland

Since 2003 ACPCs in Northern Ireland have had responsibility to undertake Case Management Reviews (CMR) (similar to SCRs in England and Wales) where a child dies, including death by suicide, and abuse or neglect is known, or suspected, to be a factor in the child's death. They are also asked to consider undertaking a CMR where a child has sustained a potentially life-threatening injury through abuse (including sexual abuse) or neglect; has sustained serious and permanent impairment of health or development through abuse or neglect; or the case gives rise to concerns about the way in which local professionals and services worked together to safeguard children. Chapter 10 of *Co-operating to Safeguard Children* (Department of Health, Social Services and Public Safety, 2003) provides guidance on when and how a CMR should be undertaken. The circumstances under which a review should take place are similar to those in England and Wales but the Northern Ireland guidance does not specifically state that a CMR should be undertaken where a parent has been murdered and a homicide review is being initiated, or where a child has been killed by a parent with a mental illness. The guidance states that reviews should normally be completed within five months. It says little about the involvement of families in the review process except that the ACPC chair should consider whether family members should be invited to contribute to the review.

In Northern Ireland ACPCs have to provide a copy of the review report to the Department of Health, Social Services and Public Safety (DHSSPS) which is responsible for identifying and disseminating common themes and trends. *Co-operating to Safeguard Children* (Department of Health, Social Services and Public Safety, 2003) states that the Department will commission regional case management overview reports which will be published at intervals to maximise learning. Researchers from Queen's University and the NSPCC recently evaluated the operation of the CMR process in Northern Ireland.

Significant Case Reviews in Scotland

While local safeguarding bodies in England and Wales have undertaken case reviews when a child dies and abuse or neglect is known, or suspected, to be a factor in the child's death, for many years there was no equivalent procedure in Scotland. Prior to 2007 there was no single system of notification, no agreed criteria for inclusion and no national system of review. The duty for local authorities to cooperate was, however, mandated in the Children (Scotland) Act 1995 and ministers could order an inquiry if they thought it was necessary (Galilee, 2005; Axford and Bullock, 2005). There were a number of approaches for undertaking reviews into significant cases but no standard approach. Some local areas, usually through CPCs, did undertake reviews of professional practice following deaths of children known to agencies, and where there were concerns about abuse or neglect reviews of significant cases were sometimes undertaken by agencies involved in child protection, whether singly or jointly. Local areas and individual agencies had their own processes and procedures in place and across Scotland there was a degree of inconsistency in how decisions were made about when to call for a review; what type of review to hold; the management of the process; the skills and expertise required to undertake the review; the reporting requirements of the review; and the implementation of the findings (Axford and Bullock, 2005).

Processes for investigating child deaths/serious cases in Scotland before 2007

🖺 Fatal Accident Inquiries (FAIs) were conducted where children died in custody or where the Procurator Fiscal decided an inquiry was in the public interest.

🖺 The deaths of all children who died while looked after were reviewed by local authorities and the Scottish Executive and were the subject of a statutory report to ministers.

🖺 Neonatal deaths were reviewed where there was an unexplained death of a child under two.

🖺 Some local areas, usually through Child Protection Committees (CPCs), undertook reviews of professional practice following deaths of children known to agencies or where there were concerns about abuse and neglect.

🖺 Agencies also had their own internal review arrangements for significant cases or incidents. (Axford and Bullock, 2005)

The report of the National Audit and Review of Child Protection in Scotland *It's Everyone's Job to Make Sure I'm Alright* (Scottish Executive, 2002) recommended that the Scottish Executive consider the need for guidance on how reviews of child fatalities should be conducted. A Child Death and Significant Case Review Group was established as part of the Child Protection Reform Programme and extensive consultation took place during 2006 on draft guidance for conducting significant incident reviews. A study of international comparisons of child death review processes was commissioned to inform the review group (Axford and Bullock, 2005).

Interim Guidance for Child Protection Committees (CPCs) for Conducting a Significant Case Review was published in 2007 to provide a systematic and transparent approach to the review process (Scottish Executive, 2007). The grounds for undertaking a Significant Case Review are similar to those for undertaking an SCR in England and Wales but do not include where a parent has been murdered and a homicide review is being initiated. Neither does the guidance specifically state that a review should be undertaken where a child has been killed by a parent with a mental illness though this is presumably covered by 'death by alleged murder or culpable homicide'.

Circumstances which might warrant a Significant Case Review in Scotland

WHEN A CHILD DIES AND:

🖺 abuse and neglect is known or suspected to be a factor in the child's death;

🖺 the child is on, or has been on, the Child Protection Register (CPR) or a sibling is or was on the CPR;

🖺 the death is by suicide or accidental death;

🖺 the death is by alleged murder, culpable homicide, reckless conduct, or act of violence;

🖺 the child was looked after by the local authority;

📑 **and**, in addition to this, the incident or accumulation of incidents (a case) gives rise to serious concerns about professional and/or service involvement or lack of involvement.

WHEN A CHILD HAS NOT DIED BUT

📑 has sustained significant harm or risk of significant harm, under one or more of the categories of abuse and neglect set out in *Protecting Children – A Shared Responsibility: Guidance for Inter-Agency Co-operation*. Bear in mind that cumulative inaction or wrong action may be more difficult to evidence but nevertheless should be considered to the best extent possible);

📑 **and**, in addition to this, the incident or accumulation of incidents (a case) gives rise to serious concerns about professional and/or service involvement or lack of involvement.

There is a section in the guidance on the involvement of family/carers which states that the family/carers of the child should be kept informed at various stages of the review. It suggests that it may be useful to assign a member of staff to be a liaison point for the family and their role could include making arrangements to interview the child, family/carers or significant adults involved. Scotland is the only part of the UK where guidance states that the extent of family/carers' involvement should be documented as well as whether the child's views and wishes were sought and expressed. There is also a useful section in the guidance on supporting staff through the review process which is not found in the guidance in other parts of the UK.

Timescales for completion of a review are not given in the Scottish guidance but it states that for every case the CPC should agree a deadline for when reports should be produced in the light of the circumstances and context of that particular case. It also states that there is an assumption that the CPC will proceed as speedily as is feasible through the various processes of review.

The guidance states that CPCs should produce a summary of cases sent to them over the course of the year and introduce these into the learning cycle, whether the decision was to undertake a Significant Case Review or not (Scottish Executive, 2007). CPCs are also asked to send summaries of cases to the government as some recommendations for reviews may be for consideration at national level. The Guidance also states that the government will circulate reports to inspectorates and communicate with organisations such as universities and colleges, NHS Education, and regulatory bodies such as the Scottish Social Services Council if recommendations from reviews have implications for them. There has, however, been no analysis of the findings from Significant Case Reviews across Scotland as there has been in England and Wales and inspectorates do not evaluate reviews as they do in England. Whether or not CPCs have involved families in the process and recorded the extent of their involvement and whether or not staff have been supported through the review process is not, therefore, known. Neither is it known whether reviews in Scotland take longer to complete than in other parts of the UK because of the absence of timescales in the guidance.

WIDER CHILD DEATH REVIEW PROCESSES

Background

In addition to processes for reviewing deaths from child abuse and neglect some parts of the UK have recently introduced, or plan to introduce, processes for wider review of child deaths in an attempt to expand child death review beyond the focus of child abuse and neglect to one of public health. Evidence presented in the CEMACH child death review study (Pearson, 2008) suggests that a public health approach might be a more effective way of learning. The study concluded that half of the deaths which panels considered might have been avoided would not have been identified as 'unexpected' under the 'Working Together' definition, highlighting the need to review all child deaths rather than just unexpected ones.

Countries such as the US, Canada and Australia have had wider child death review processes for some years. Child fatality review teams were first developed in the US because of concerns about the under-reporting of child abuse deaths. The first documented multi-agency and systematic response to child deaths appears to have been initiated in 1978 by Los Angeles County. Since 1978 child death review processes have spread across the US and by 2007 all but one state had established a child death review team (Bunting and Reid, 2005; Axford and Bullock, 2005).

Until recently no parts of the UK had wider child death review processes equivalent to those in the US and some Canadian and Australian states. There have, however, always been health-based approaches to infant and child mortality review in the UK and there is a long-established history of hospital mortality reviews. Hospitals regularly carry out audits or internal reviews of some, but not all, child deaths.

England

As well as having a statutory responsibility to undertake SCRs, since 1 April 2008, LSCBs in England have two new interrelated responsibilities in relation to review of child deaths.

New child death review responsibilities for LSCBs in England

- LSCBs have a duty to review all child deaths from 0 to 18 in a systematic way through a Child Death Overview Panel (CDOP);

📰 LSCBs have a duty to respond rapidly to individual unexpected deaths of all children, not just those in contact with organisations responsible for safeguarding their welfare, in the local authority area, through a rapid response team (RRT).

In addition, LSCBs also have a statutory responsibility to use the aggregated findings from all child deaths, collected according to a nationally agreed data set, to inform local strategic planning on how best to safeguard and promote the welfare of children in their area. An unexpected death is defined as a death 'which was not anticipated as a significant possibility 24 hours before the death or where there was a similarly unexpected collapse leading to or precipitating the events which led to the death' (HM Government, 2006).

The overall purpose of these new child death review processes is to understand why children die and put in place interventions to protect other children and prevent future deaths.

Chapter 7 of *Working Together to Safeguard Children* (HM Government, 2006) sets out the new processes for reviewing child deaths, setting the scene for England to become the first country in the world to have national standards and procedures for the investigation and management of unexpected child deaths and for reviewing all deaths (Sidebotham *et al.*, 2008). The guidelines in *Working Together* were based on the findings of the Kennedy Report into the management of SUDI (RCPATH and RCPCH, 2004), which was convened after three high-profile infant death prosecutions failed. The government announced it would set up these new processes in its response to the inquiry into the death of Victoria Climbie. Prior to these new processes it was likely that only a minority of child deaths received a post-mortem and an even smaller number were accorded a public inquest but this information is not actually known since a breakdown of figures is not available by age from the Registrar General's Office. Figures are available in Northern Ireland where only 20% of child deaths receive a post-mortem and just 13% are subject to a public inquest (Bunting and Reid, 2005).

Wales

LSCBs in Wales were not given responsibilities to review all child deaths from 0 to 18 or to respond rapidly to individual unexpected deaths of all children as LSCBs in England were under the Children Act 2004. Because the population base of LSCBs in Wales is significantly less than the recommended 500,000 for child death review arrangements in England, the Welsh Assembly Government has instead been investigating whether an all-Wales approach would be a more feasible way of administering child death reviews. The Welsh

Assembly Government's Safeguarding Group has proposed arrangements for the setting up and running of a pilot study to inform the development of child death reviews in Wales. The pilot began in Autumn 2008 and will run for 18 months with the aim of introducing a full Child Death Scheme from 1 April 2010.

Northern Ireland

New child death review processes are also being considered in Northern Ireland in response to a CMR following the death of David Briggs, a twin adopted in Romania, in 2003. The CMR report recommended a multi-agency approach be used in all cases of sudden unexpected child death in Northern Ireland.

Scotland

At the time of writing (June 2009) the Scottish Government has not announced plans to introduce new processes for wider review of child deaths.

THE EFFECTIVENESS OF INQUIRY AND REVIEW PROCESSES

Case review processes were intended to be used as a learning tool, not as a means of attributing blame, and in most parts of the UK attempts have been made to aggregate the findings from case reviews so that there can be national as well as local learning. The fact that SCRs continue to identify the same problems in front-line practice and continue to make similar recommendations has, however, raised questions about their effectiveness as a learning tool for improving practice. The Ofsted (2008a) evaluation concluded that SCRs were effective at identifying what happened to children but less effective at addressing why it happened. It was critical of the fact that recommendations tended to focus on policies and procedures as opposed to practice and what needed to change. Rose and Barnes (2008) also found that SCR recommendations focused predominantly on procedures.

Rose and Barnes (2008) point out that it is important to bear in mind that SCRs are only one source of evidence about what is happening in work to safeguard children. While child deaths are comparatively rare, writers such as Parton (2004) and Masson (2006) suggest that they have had an inordinate and inappropriate level of influence on safeguarding policy. Masson (2006) has commented that 'Understanding what went wrong is a limited activity to which only modest resources should be committed'.

Rose and Barnes (2008) argue that approaches which enable us to learn from effective safeguarding practice, rather than mistakes, would be a far better way to proceed. The Social Care Institute for Excellence (SCIE) has developed an alternative approach to case review (Fish *et al.*, 2008) – a resource for undertaking a multi-agency systems approach for organisational learning across agencies involved in safeguarding children. The approach, which is widely used in engineering, health and other high risk industries, provides the opportunity to study the whole system so we can learn from what is working effectively as well as from what is not working well.

While SCRs can provide useful information about child abuse and neglect deaths, 'The challenge is to expand child death reviews beyond the focus of child abuse and neglect to one of public health so as to identify preventable child deaths and achieve effective prevention' (Onwuachi-Saunders *et al.*, 1999, p. 278).

New processes for wider child death review are an attempt to do just this. The Sidebotham *et al.* (2008) pilot study provides some evidence of how new child death review processes in England are operating. Nine LSCBs who responded to an initial questionnaire were selected as sites for further research. CDOPs were at an early stage of development when the pilot study was undertaken but a number of outcomes were already being observed such as public awareness campaigns, community safety initiatives, training of professionals, development of protocols and lobbying of politicians. Further evidence of the effectiveness of child death review in the UK comes from the CEMACH child death review study (Pearson, 2008). The CEMACH study was a pilot study to determine whether confidential enquiry methodology could be used to identify avoidable factors in child deaths. The CEMACH study concluded that confidential enquiry methodology could be effectively used to determine whether the deaths of children could have been avoided. Interestingly the study included two consultation sessions with 24 young people aged 14 to 20. After reviewing three child death cases the young people felt they needed a greater awareness of danger in their lives, particularly with regard to substance misuse and traffic accidents.

Although the Sidebotham study provided some evidence of the effectiveness of new child death review processes it also identified a number of problems. One of the main problems was that none of the nine overview panels in the pilot had managed to set up a foolproof system of notification. Most sites commented that current systems for notification of deaths were inadequate and they reported that they had to rely on a combination of sources: Child

Surveillance Teams or Decision Support Teams of the Primary Care Trusts; coroners; the police; children's social care; public health; hospital records departments; and registrars. Notification of deaths of children who lived in one area but who died outside this area was particularly problematic. One LSCB reported that they received notifications of all child deaths from a tertiary hospital in their area regardless of the child's place of residence. These concerns could prove to be significant since evidence suggests that 40% of deaths of children under one and between a quarter and a third of deaths of older children occur outside the area in which the child resided, making local ascertainment of death problematic (Ward Platt, 2007).

Participants in the Sidebotham *et al.* (2008) study cited various systems for review of children's deaths - local case discussions for SUDI, local case discussions for other unexpected child deaths, infant mortality reviews in hospital and by the perinatal unit, other hospital mortality reviews and domestic violence reviews – but reported that there was not a consistent process. The nine sites all had protocols for responding to unexpected childhood deaths, many of which had been operational for several years, but most covered only unexpected deaths of children under two. There were some concerns about reviewing all deaths from 0 to 18, particularly in relation to the neonatal period and later adolescent period, since different professionals are involved with the older and younger age groups. In many sites there was already some sort of hospital-based neonatal mortality review and the challenge was to try to include them in the CDOP process rather than replace an already well-functioning system. Some teams were dividing deaths into categories and reviewing all deaths within one category at a time to enable appropriate expertise to be brought in to support the panel. While there was a general sense of enthusiasm for developing child death review processes there was some frustration at the perceived lack of central guidance other than that set out in *Working Together.*

Working Together (HM Government, 2006) requires LSCBs to establish CDOPs for populations greater than 500,000 and states that neighbouring LSCBs could form combined CDOPs to achieve this population size. Sidebotham *et al.* (2008) found that some panels were planning to develop a combined CDOP but others were not keen to do so even where population numbers were low. They found that teams could function with both smaller and larger populations and concluded that LSCBs should consider what configuration best met their needs. Ward Platt (2007) states, however, that from his experience in the North of England (a participating region in the CEMACH child death project), it makes sense for adjacent LSCBs to pool expertise and cover larger populations than their own. He suggests populations of between 500,000 and a million would allow a reasonable number of deaths to be scrutinised each year without the process becoming too burdensome.

Working Together (HM Government, 2006) includes a diagram to explain the interface between child death and SCR but Sidebotham *et al.* (2008) found there were problems around linkage of the two processes. There was a clear message from interviewees that SCRs were intensive, demanding and time-consuming and that child death review processes could not, and should not, go into the same kind of depth. Participants were also unclear about the distinction between child death overview processes and rapid response processes. They talked about the differences between the multi-agency child death overview and other hospital-based mortality reviews that were already being undertaken in many places and generally considered that the CDOP should consider cases only after the conclusion of any rapid response process, criminal investigation or SCR.

The CEMACH study report (Pearson, 2008) argues that there needs to be consistency and standardisation across LSCBs and aggregation at a regional and national level if major issues and trends in child mortality are to be identified. It also points out that enquiry staff who were involved in the CEMACH study found the emotional content of their work demanding and stressful at times. This is likely to apply to staff involved in reviews in LSCBs as well and the report states that it will be important to ensure they are appropriately supported. Accountability is another issue that the report suggests requires further clarification. It asks to whom CDOP decisions on contributory factors are accountable and who is responsible if recommendations for prevention are made but not carried through (if, for example, children continue to die from preventable road accidents).

There is a growing body of evidence on the effectiveness of child death review processes in other countries but much of it relates to activity stemming from the process rather than specific outcomes for children. Bunting and Reid (2005) identified a number of benefits including improved multi-agency working and communication; more effective identification of suspicious cases and a decrease in inadequate death certificates; a more complete and accountable process and a more in-depth understanding of the causes of child death from a narrow and stigmatising focus on child abuse towards a public health model that focuses on the prevention of all deaths.

In the US and Australia comprehensive child death review programmes have contributed significantly to knowledge about child abuse and neglect. Knowledge from child death review has led to policies and initiatives that have made major contributions to keeping children safe, such as the fencing of domestic pools and the use of child cycle helmets. In Arizona the Child Death Review Team supported increased enforcement and community education regarding Arizona's child safety restraint laws, including legislation establishing a graduated driver's licence programme for teens (Rimsza *et al.*, 2002). In Philadelphia as a result of information from child death reviews school nurses received training in domestic abuse, there has been enforcement of child safety seat law, recognition of the need for Fire Starter programmes for children aged three to seven, and recognition of the need for non-battery powered smoke detectors (Onwuachi-Saunders *et al.*, 1999). Evidence from child death reviews can also be used to identify special population groups that need targeted prevention programmes. For example, the Arizona Child Death Review Team found that unintentional injury deaths and suicide were more common in Native American communities, whereas deaths attributable to gunshot wounds occurred more frequently in Hispanic communities (Rimsza *et al.*, 2002).

Child death review teams in the US have, however, faced a number of difficulties. One of the main challenges has been the difficulty of obtaining and sustaining adequate resources and many teams have reported an inability to expand their focus or put prevention programmes into place (Durfee *et al.*, 2002). Lack of national leadership and co-ordination has meant there is wide variation in child death review team organisation and processes across the US and there are no national criteria by which programme structure and impact might be judged (Webster *et al.*, 2003). There are no standardised methods of data collection across teams so comparability of child deaths between states and the identification of national trends is impossible (Bunting and Reid, 2005).

CONCLUSION

This chapter outlined the processes and mechanisms currently operating in Scotland and other parts of the UK to review child deaths and cases of significant abuse. The main findings are:

❏ Finding out what happened when a child dies is a basic human right now enshrined in the Human Rights Act 1998.

❏ Statutory inquiries ordered by governments are rare; in most cases reviews are commissioned at local level through local safeguarding bodies.

❏ The purpose of review is to examine the role of agencies who were involved in the case, establish whether any lessons can be learned and make recommendations to improve practice.

❏ CPCs/LSCBs in England and Wales have had responsibilities to undertake SCRs for 20 years; only since 2004 has this been a statutory duty.

❏ ACPCs in Northern Ireland have had responsibility to undertake CMRs since 2003.

❏ CPCs in Scotland have had responsibility to undertake Significant Case Reviews since 2007.

❏ There is no statutory duty to undertake case reviews in Scotland or Northern Ireland.

❏ Since 2008 LSCBs in England have also had a statutory duty to review all child deaths from 0 to 18 through a CDOP and to respond rapidly to individual unexpected deaths of all children through an RRT; Wales and Northern Ireland are also planning to introduce processes for wider review of child deaths.

❏ Evidence from other countries suggests that wider review of all child deaths might be a more effective way of enabling identification of the causes of child death and may lead to the introduction of policies and initiatives to prevent some deaths.

❏ In the UK new processes for review of all child deaths sit alongside processes for review of deaths from child abuse and neglect, as well as other health-based processes for review of child deaths, and there is a need to ensure that these separate processes fit together.

This chapter and the preceding chapter set the scene by providing contextual information about the number and cause of child deaths in the UK and the processes for inquiring into and reviewing child deaths. The following three chapters focus on key public inquiries and reviews into child deaths and serious cases in Scotland. Chapter 3 provides information in relation to key cases in Scotland and looks at the type of inquiry or review undertaken in relation to these cases.

CHAPTER 3

Key public inquiries and reviews

Introduction

Much has been written about inquiries or reviews into child deaths and serious abuse but most of the available information relates to cases in England and Wales. This chapter and Chapters 4 and 5 set out information about key public inquiries and reviews into child deaths and serious cases in Scotland. This chapter identifies cases in Scotland where one or more child or young person (aged 18 or under) was killed or abused and there was an inquiry or review process resulting in a publicly available report. It looks at the type of inquiry or review undertaken, the methods that were used and the format of the inquiry/review report produced, and considers the nature of the case that was investigated.

Key Scottish public inquiries and reviews

- The Report of the Committee of Inquiry into the consideration given and steps taken towards securing the welfare of **Richard Clark** by Perth Town Council and other bodies or persons concerned (1975)
- The Report of the Inquiry into the Removal of Children from **Orkney** in February 1991 (1992)
- The Public Inquiry into the Shootings at **Dunblane** Primary School on 13 March 1996 (1996)
- Edinburgh's Children: The Report of the **Edinburgh** Inquiry into Abuse and Protection of Children in Care (1999)
- The Child Protection Inquiry into the Circumstances Surrounding the Death of **Kennedy McFarlane**, d.o.b. 17 April 1997 (2001)
- **Fife** Council Independent Enquiry Established by the Chief Executive Following the Conviction of David Logan Murphy for the Sexual Abuse of Children (2002)
- The Report of the **Caleb Ness** Inquiry (2003)
- The Child Review report into the life and death of **Carla Nicole Bone** 07-04-01 – 13-05-02 (2003)
- An Inspection into the Care and Protection of Children in **Eilean Siar** (2005)

- The Review of the Management Arrangements of **Colyn Evans** by Fife Constabulary and Fife Council (2005)
- Independent Review into the Circumstances surrounding the death of **Danielle Reid** (2006)
- **Historical Abuse Systemic Review**, Residential Schools and Children's Homes in Scotland 1950 to 1995 (2007)
- Independent Inquiry into Abuse at **Kerelaw** Residential School and Secure Unit (2009)

TYPE OF INQUIRY/REVIEW

The key public inquiry and review reports into child deaths and significant abuse in Scotland are outlined in the box above. The earliest public inquiry or review report in Scotland was published in 1975, the most recent in 2009. It is interesting that no Scottish inquiries or reviews into child deaths or significant abuse were undertaken between 1975 and 1990. This is in marked contrast to England and Wales where there were many inquiries or reviews into child deaths and abuse over this period (Galilee, 2005).

The Richard Clark, Orkney and Dunblane inquiries were ordered by a Secretary of State for Scotland. The Richard Clark Inquiry was not a statutory inquiry because, like the Maria Colwell Inquiry in England which took place just before it, it was undertaken prior to the 1975 Children Act and had no statutory powers to compel people to attend. The Inquiry was held in private but names were included in the report. Orkney and Dunblane were statutory inquiries undertaken in the 1990s. The proceedings were held in public and the witnesses who gave evidence did so under oath or affirmation. Most of the witnesses in the Orkney Inquiry were represented by their own QC, with around 15 QCs involved in the Inquiry. The Dunblane Inquiry, chaired by Lord Cullen in 1996, was a Tribunal constituted under Section 1 of the Tribunals of Inquiry (Evidence) Act 1921.

The Edinburgh Inquiry in 1999 was the first inquiry to be held under the Children (Scotland) Act 1995. The Edinburgh Inquiry was somewhat unusual in that it had the full range of powers of a statutory inquiry but took a less adversarial line than that taken by most other statutory inquiries. The panel for the Edinburgh Inquiry took evidence in private and names were not revealed in the report, with the exception of the names of those who had already been convicted. The focus of the inquiry was more on the welfare of the children than on an attempt to attribute blame. Corby *et al.* (2001) have contrasted the Edinburgh Inquiry, and its focus on the needs of the victims, with the North Wales Tribunal and its focus on guilt and culpability.

The Historical Abuse Systemic Review was commissioned by the Scottish Parliament. It followed a debate held in the Scottish Parliament on 1 December 2004. The debate was a motion on behalf of the Public Petitions Committee, seeking an inquiry into past institutional child abuse. No individuals or organisations were named in the report.

Fife, Kennedy McFarlane, Caleb Ness, Carla Nicole Bone, and Danielle Reid were independent inquiries or reviews. They were all commissioned by Child Protection Committees or local authorities between 2000 and 2006. As outlined in Chapter 2, Scotland never had Part 8 reviews, and national guidance on the conduct of Significant Case Reviews was not issued until 2007. Despite this a number of the reviews into child death or significant abuse that were undertaken by CPCs were carried out in a similar way to Serious Case Reviews in England and Wales. The authors of the Caleb Ness Inquiry report stated that they closely followed the Part 8 review format in England and Wales, as did the author of the Danielle Reid review report. A significant difference, however, is that the Caleb Ness Inquiry report and Danielle Reid review report were made public whereas Part 8 Reviews/SCRs in England and Wales are anonymous, although LSCBs are required to publish executive summaries. Children have been named in most of these Scottish reports but staff are not normally named.

The Independent Inquiry into Abuse at Kerelaw Residential School and Secure Unit was commissioned by the Scottish Government and Glasgow City Council in 2007. It took place in private and all information in the report was anonymised.

> We also decided that we were more likely to have productive engagement with those who were willing to give evidence if we followed the example of the Edinburgh Inquiry by adopting an inquisitorial rather than an adversarial approach to interviewing. Our aim was to understand individuals' experiences of Kerelaw, and to address key themes in as open-ended a way as possible. This allowed those we interviewed to talk about their involvement with Kerelaw in their own way. (Frizzell, p.14)

Two of the more recent publicly available reviews into child deaths or abuse in Scotland have been undertaken by inspection agencies. The review of the management arrangements in the case of Colyn Evans was requested by Scottish Ministers following considerable public and media interest about what was covered in a local review of the case. The review was undertaken by the

Social Work Inspection Agency (SWIA) and Her Majesty's Inspectorate of Constabulary (HMIC). The SWIA was also asked by Comhairle Nan Eilean Siar (the Western Isles Council) to undertake the review into the care and protection of children in Eilean Siar (the Western Isles).

METHODS

In terms of methods, most of the Scottish inquiries and reviews involved interviewing people who were involved in the case and analysing the records of the agencies concerned. For example:

- SWIA commented that they read and analysed 220,000 pages of material for the Eilean Siar review. They chose not to interview staff in the agencies concerned because the police had already conducted an extensive criminal investigation which involved interviewing a large number of witnesses.

- The Caleb Ness Inquiry team interviewed 37 witnesses. They were also given all the documents which were produced at Alexander Ness's trial, including medical records, social work records, criminal justice records and police interviews.

- There were 26 witnesses in the Richard Clark Inquiry and written representations from two professional bodies; 13 documents were produced.

- Forty-nine witnesses were interviewed for the Danielle Reid review and two formal written reports were received. Documents were also analysed.

- Sixteen former residents, 42 former members of staff and one of the abusers were interviewed for the Edinburgh Inquiry. Another former resident was contacted through a professional associated with him and 15 other former staff members were contacted by telephone or letter. The inquiry team were also in contact with one elected member.

- The Kerelaw Inquiry read records of interviews by Council investigators with over 90 residents or former residents of Kerelaw and over 100 employees or former employees, plus reports of investigations and records of subsequent disciplinary proceedings and files held by HMIE, SWIA, and the Care Commission. 55 former Kerelaw employees and 35 current or former Council managers were interviewed. 22 ex-residents provided oral evidence and a further two provided written evidence and two parents of young people who had been in Kerelaw were interviewed. Oral or written evidence was also provided by Children's Rights Officers, individuals from local authorities other than Glasgow who had placed young people in Kerelaw, the Scottish Government, unions, Inspectorates and others.

THE FORMAT OF INQUIRY/REVIEW REPORTS

The format of Scottish inquiry and review reports varies considerably (see Table 3.1 below). The report for the Richard Clark Inquiry, which was published in 1975, was only 43 pages long. It had a conclusions section but did not make recommendations. In contrast the Orkney Inquiry was 363 pages long and made 194 recommendations.

Inquiry and review reports have similarly varied considerably in other parts of the UK. Some reports are very long with a large number of recommendations, while others are only a few pages. The Maria Colwell Inquiry report in 1975 was 120 pages but more recent inquiry reports have tended to be much longer – the North Wales Tribunal report was over 900 pages long and made 72 recommendations and the Victoria Climbie report was 400 pages long and had 108 recommendations (Reder and Duncan 2004; Corby *et al.*, 2001). Owers *et al.* (1999) reviewed 10 SCRs in Wales and found that the total number of pages ranged from 33 to 557 and the total number of recommendations from seven to 74. Across the 10 cases there was a positive correlation between the number of pages and the number of recommendations, with the longer reports containing more recommendations. In a second review of 10 cases in Wales Brandon *et al.* (2002) found that the number of pages ranged from 33 to 549, but in contrast to the 1999 study, the number of recommendations (between six and 49) did not correlate with the number of pages.

Table 3.1 Length of Scottish reports and number of recommendations

Report	Number of pages	Number of recommendations
Richard Clark	43	0
Orkney	363	194
Dunblane	174	28
Edinburgh	287	135
Fife	78	41
Kennedy McFarlane	42	33
Caleb Ness	264	35
Carla Nicole Bone	85	37
Eilean Siar	162	31
Danielle Reid	196	68
Colyn Evans	45	20
Historic abuse systemic review	279	8
Kerelaw	154	38

THE NATURE OF THE CASE

The key Scottish inquiry and review reports include cases where children died or were seriously harmed, or were allegedly seriously harmed, in the home as well as cases relating to child deaths or significant abuse in the community.

CHILD DEATH OR SERIOUS ABUSE IN THE HOME

Richard Clark, Kennedy McFarlane, Caleb Ness, Carla Nicole Bone and Danielle Reid were either killed or suffered significant abuse in the home. Kennedy McFarlane, Caleb Ness, Carla Nicole Bone and Danielle Reid all died. Richard Clark did not die but his injuries were so severe that he never recovered.

The Eilean Siar case is somewhat different because it involved the abuse of more than one child, there was more than one perpetrator, and none of the alleged perpetrators was actually convicted. Nine adults, including family members and friends of the family, were originally charged in relation to the abuse of eight children in two separate families but all charges were subsequently dropped when the Crown Office decided not to proceed with the case. SWIA concluded there was no evidence to suggest the five children in the family they referred to as Family B were abused but they concluded that the three children in Family A had experienced severe and prolonged abuse.

The Orkney Inquiry in 1991 inquired into the removal of nine children from their homes on South Ronaldsay following allegations of sexual abuse by children from another family. The Orkney Inquiry did not inquire into whether any abuse actually took place, and no abuse was ever proven. In some respects the Orkney case was similar to the Eilean Siar case because it involved the alleged abuse of a number of children from a number of families by their parents and family friends and the families lived in a small island community. In other respects Orkney is, however, unique. Lord Clyde, the chair of the Orkney Inquiry, himself stated that 'The case of the nine Orkney children is in some respects special'.

The case involved four families who lived on the island of South Ronaldsay. In 1991 nine children from the four families were removed to places of safety by social workers with the assistance of police officers. The removal of the children followed allegations of organised sexual abuse made during interviews with children from another family. The matter was referred to the Children's Hearings and the children were accommodated for two months when, following a decision in the Sheriff court that the proceedings to prove the grounds for referral were incompetent, they were returned home. The Inquiry that followed was not concerned with establishing whether any abuse had taken place; instead its remit was to inquire into the decision made by

Orkney Islands Council and the Northern Constabulary to remove the children from their homes, a decision which received significant criticism. The case probably bears most resemblance to the Cleveland Inquiry in England which took place a few years prior to the Orkney Inquiry (Secretary of State for Social Services, 1988).

CHILD DEATHS IN THE COMMUNITY

The Dunblane Inquiry and Colyn Evans review relate to child deaths in the community. The Colyn Evans report considers issues connected with the management of a young person who had been looked after by Fife Council. Colyn Evans killed 16-year-old Karen Dewar, who lived in the same neighbourhood as himself, when he was 17. He was known to have a history of sexually aggressive behaviour, had been subject to supervision by Fife Council and was still receiving throughcare support. As a juvenile he had been dealt with under the Children's Hearing system and could not, therefore, be registered as a sex offender but he had been classified as a non-registered sex offender. The judge at Colyn Evans's trial stated that the facts of the murder of Karen Dewar would not require Colyn Evans to register as a sex offender on his release from prison.

The Dunblane Inquiry inquired into the deaths of 18 people, including 16 children, at Dunblane Primary School. Thomas Hamilton entered Dunblane Primary School and killed and shot teacher Gwen Mayor and 16 of her Primary 1 class. He also inflicted gunshot wounds on 10 other pupils and three other members of the teaching staff before shooting himself. He was not a known sex offender and had never been charged with any crime but a number of concerns had been raised about him in connection with his relationships with boys.

ABUSE IN RESIDENTIAL CARE

Four of the inquiries and reviews relate to cases of abuse in residential care. The Edinburgh Inquiry was a historical abuse case relating to the sexual abuse of large numbers of children in two children's homes by two staff members over a period of 14 years. It followed the conviction of two former residential care workers in 1997 of serious sexual abuse of children between 1973 and 1983. Gordon Knott was sentenced to 16 years for crimes committed at Clerwood and Glenallan children's homes. Brian McLennan was sentenced to 11 years for crimes committed at Clerwood and Dean House children's homes (his sentence was later reduced to six years after appeal). Clerwood and Glenallan were local authority homes; Dean House was a voluntary home. The two men worked together briefly at Clerwood but no evidence was found to suggest they were part of any kind of 'paedophile ring'. The Inquiry investigated whether victims' complaints had been properly handled in the past, how adequate procedures were at the time to protect children and what further safeguards were needed.

The Fife Enquiry followed the conviction of David Logan Murphy in 2001 on 30 charges of sexual abuse of children in residential care from 1959 to 1989. Allegations had been made against him in the early 1970s but he had not been prosecuted. Fife Council set up an independent enquiry following his conviction to consider what lessons the council should learn and to propose any changes needed to minimise the risks to children being abused while in public care; to identify what action was taken when children made complaints of abuse at the time; and to review the internal social work audit undertaken in Fife of measures to protect children.

The Historical Abuse Systemic Review was an inquiry into past institutional child abuse suffered by children in residential schools and children's homes across Scotland between 1950 and 1995. The review was about systems not individuals. It looked at the systems of laws, rules and regulations that governed residential schools and children's homes; it did not report on the facts or circumstances of individual cases of abuse.

The Independent Inquiry into Abuse at Kerelaw Residential School and Secure Unit followed internal investigations by Glasgow City Council and a separate police inquiry. Twenty-one individuals were reported to the Procurator Fiscal, mostly for physical abuse. The police inquiry resulted in two convictions, one of a teacher and one of a unit manager, on charges of physical and sexual abuse. The Inquiry did not examine individual allegations of abuse or investigate whether abuse had occurred. Its purpose was to investigate the circumstances that led to emotional, physical and sexual abuse of residents at Kerelaw, to examine Glasgow City Council's stewardship of the school since 1996, and to consider the Council's investigation of what occurred and the arrangements following closure of the school between 2004 and 2006. The Inquiry was asked to make recommendations to ensure similar circumstances could not arise again and to offer any insights relevant to the safe care of young people in residential settings.

CONCLUSION

This chapter identified key cases in Scotland where one or more child or young person (aged 18 or under) was killed or abused and there was some sort of inquiry or review process resulting in a publicly available report. It looked at the type of inquiry or review undertaken, the methods used, the format of the inquiry or review report produced, and the nature of the case which was investigated. It found that:

- ❏ there were 13 key public inquiries or reviews into child death or abuse in Scotland between 1975 and 2009;
- ❏ the inquiries and reviews were ordered by a Secretary of State or the Scottish Parliament, or commissioned by Child Protection Committees (CPCs) or local authorities;
- ❏ the format of inquiry and review reports varies considerably: the number of pages ranges from 42 to 363; the number of recommendations ranges from 0 to 194;
- ❏ 7 reports relate to the death or abuse of children in the home;
- ❏ 2 reports relate to the death of children in the community;
- ❏ 4 concern abuse in residential care.

Chapter 4 considers child, family and environmental themes that can be identified in the 13 cases that were identified in this chapter.

Child, family and environmental themes

Introduction

This chapter and the following chapter consider the main themes that can be identified in the inquiries and reviews into child deaths and significant cases in Scotland identified in the previous chapter. Because the number of inquiries and reviews in Scotland is relatively small, information from inquiries and reviews into child deaths and serious cases in England and Wales are also referred to, to provide some comparison and to corroborate the Scottish data. Case studies and learning points are used to illustrate the meaning of these themes for child care practitioners. The themes which have been identified can be divided into child, family and environmental themes and agency themes. Child, family and environmental themes are discussed in this chapter and agency themes are discussed in Chapter 5.

When considering the findings presented in this chapter it is important to remember that the information available to an inquiry or review is only ever partial. A number of researchers have pointed out that many inquiry reports lack basic and essential information (Reder *et al.*, 1993; Cooper, 2005; Owers *et al.*, 1999; Brandon *et al.*, 2002), making it difficult to present a comprehensive picture of the families involved in these cases. Many of the Scottish inquiry and review reports similarly lack important information making it difficult to form a complete picture of the perpetrators, their victims and their families. The age of parents, age of siblings, information about the perpetrators' own childhoods and information about their socio-economic circumstances are frequently missing.

Prevention of child death and serious abuse requires professionals to prioritise the most serious and concerning cases but understanding what characteristics of family relationships might place children at increased risk of death or serious abuse is complex. Poverty, mental health problems, alcohol and drug misuse, and exposure to maltreatment as a child are strongly associated with parents maltreating their children, but the extent to which each of these risk factors is related to the occurrence of maltreatment is hard to establish (Gilbert *et al.*, 2009). Attempts at prediction have been thwarted by limited knowledge and complexities in assessing risk (Owers *et al.*, 1999). Axford and Bullock (2005) suggest there are likely to be as many as 20 wrong predictions – false positives and false negatives – for every correct prediction.

While child death and serious abuse is hard to predict, the factors that increase the likelihood of harm are known. A number of studies have examined child death and significant abuse cases and produced an important body of evidence about risk factors (for example, DHSS, 1982; Department of Health,1991a; Reder *et al.*, 1993; Social Services Inspectorate, 1994; James, 1994; Falkov, 1996; Wilczynski, 1995; Reder and Duncan, 1999; Sanders *et al.*, 1999; Owers *et al.*, 1999; Arthurs and Ruddick, 2001; Sinclair and Bullock, 2002; Brandon *et al.*, 2002; Morris *et al.*, 2007; Rose and Barnes, 2008; Brandon *et al.*, 2008; Ofsted, 2008a; Sidebotham *et al.*, 2008), but it is important to remember that these are risk factors, as opposed to indicators of abuse (Hughes, 2009). The risk factors which have been identified have been found to be remarkably uniform across Australia, Canada, America, New Zealand, Sweden, Hong Kong and the UK (Wilczynski, 1995).

CHILD FACTORS

Age of child

Young children have been found to be most at risk of being killed or seriously abused, particularly those under the age of one (Sanders *et al.*, 1999; Reder and Duncan, 1999; Wilczynski, 1995; Schnitzer and Ewigman, 2005).

Findings from England and Wales

- 42% of cases evaluated by Ofsted (2008a) involved children under 1; 40% involved young people 11 and over.
- 47% of cases in the Brandon *et al.* (2008) study were under one; a quarter 1-5; a quarter over 11; 9% over 16.
- 29% of children in the Rose and Barnes (2008) study were under 1; 47% under 2; a fifth over 11; 13% 15 or older.
- 48% of children in the Sinclair and Bullock (2002) study were under 1; 80% under 6.
- A third of children in the Owers and Brandon (1999) study were under 1.
- Two thirds of children were babies (16 months or under) in the Brandon *et al.* (2002) study.

Of the six inquiries and reviews where children died or were significantly harmed in the home in Scotland, only Caleb Ness, 11 weeks old at the time of his death, was under one. Carla Nicole Bone was 13 months old, Richard Clark and Kennedy McFarlane were both three, Danielle Reid was five. The children in Eilean Siar were between 10 and 13 at the time the alleged perpetrators were arrested but evidence presented in the review report suggests the abuse and neglect started when the children were much younger.

Evidence from other parts of the UK suggests that older young people, particularly adolescents, may also be at increased risk. The theme of 'hard to help' older young people being failed by existing services has emerged particularly strongly in recent analyses of Serious Case Reviews in England (Brandon *et al.*, 2008; Rose and Barnes, 2008). In contrast to younger children, older young people are less likely to be killed by their parents. The majority of cases involving older young people are suicides. In nine of the 20 cases involving teenagers that Ofsted (2008a) evaluated the young person committed suicide; in three cases the young person was murdered by another young person. None of the key inquiry or review reports in Scotland relates to suicide but one involved the murder of a young person by another young person: Karen Dewar was 16 when she was murdered by 17-year-old Colyn Evans.

Gender

The findings of previous research studies have been inconclusive in terms of whether or not one gender is more likely that the other to be at risk of child death or significant abuse. Recent analyses of English Serious Case Reviews have included more boys than girls but this may be due to higher numbers of teenagers in recent studies since evidence suggests that teenage boys are significantly more likely to die than girls (Pearson, 2008).

Findings from England and Wales
- There were slightly more boys than girls (55%) in the Brandon *et al.* (2008) study.
- Almost two thirds (62%) were boys in the Rose and Barnes (2008) study.
- 60% were male in the Sinclair and Bullock (2002) study.
- 5 of the 7 children who died in the Brandon *et al.* (2002) study were male.

The Scottish cases where children have been killed or abused in the home included more girls than boys. Four of the six cases where children were killed or abused in their homes involved the death or significant abuse of girls (Kennedy McFarlane, Carla Nicole Bone, Danielle Reid and Eilean Siar), two of boys (Richard Clark and Caleb Ness).

Position in the family

Previous research (Reder and Duncan, 1999; Wilczynski, 1995) has found that children who are killed or significantly harmed are more likely to be only children or the youngest child in the family, although this may be due to the fact that very young babies are more likely to die or be seriously harmed.

Findings from England and Wales

- Over a quarter (27%) were only children in the Brandon *et al.* (2008) study; a third had one sibling; 18% came from families with 3 children; 22% lived in large families of 4 or more children; most children were the sole victim.
- A third were only children in the Sinclair and Bullock (2002) study; half were the youngest child; only 10% were the oldest.
- 4 out of 10 were the youngest child in the Owers *et al.* (1999) study; one was an only child.
- 6 out of 10 were the youngest child in the family in the Brandon *et al.* (2002) study (though 2 of these children were twins); 2 were only children.

The victims in the cases where children were killed in their homes in Scotland tended to be only children or the youngest child in their family: Caleb Ness, Danielle Reid and Carla Nicole Bone were the only children living in their household (though Caleb Ness and Carla Nicole Bone had older half-siblings living elsewhere); Kennedy McFarlane and Richard Clark were the youngest children in their household.

Disability/health problems

Victims of child death and significant abuse are often perceived to be difficult to care for by their parents and carers due to disability, health problems or behavioural problems (Sanders *et al.*, 1999; Reder *et al.*, 1993; Wilczysnki, 1995; Brandon *et al.*, 2005).

Findings from England and Wales

- A number of children in the Brandon *et al.* (2008) sample had difficult beginnings to their life: just under a fifth had spent time in a special care baby unit; disability was recorded in 5% of cases (this figure may be an underestimate since disability may not yet have been recorded in very young babies).
- 2 out of 10 children in the Brandon *et al.* (2002) study had been premature and spent time in a special care baby unit; a further 4 had learning disabilities, developmental delay or emotional/behavioural problems.
- 5 children in the 40 cases analysed by Rose and Barnes (2008) were identified as disabled; a small number of children suffered from poor health and were vulnerable as a result of being born prematurely.
- In the 40 cases analysed by Sinclair and Bullock (2002) only one child was disabled; 4 had special educational needs; 5 had significant health problems.

The authors of the Edinburgh Inquiry report commented that children with special needs were particularly vulnerable to abuse. One of the children in Eilean Siar had cerebral palsy plus a range of other disabilities. Danielle Reid and Caleb Ness both had special health needs when they were born.

> ## CASE
>
> Babies with neonatal abstinence syndrome may cry a lot, have problems feeding and be particularly demanding to care for. Caleb Ness was treated for neonatal abstinence syndrome after his birth. The authors of the Caleb Ness Inquiry report concluded that while Caleb's parents loved him and would not have harmed him deliberately they would not have been able to look after an ordinary baby, let alone one with neonatal abstinence syndrome.
>
> **Practice implication**
>
> Parents of babies with disabilities or health needs may require significant levels of support in order to be able to provide satisfactory levels of care and protection for their children.

LEARNING POINTS

✔ **Very young children are particularly vulnerable.**

✔ **Adolescents may be at increased risk.**

✔ **Only children or youngest children may be at increased risk.**

✔ **Children with disabilities or health problems may be at higher risk.**

FAMILY AND ENVIRONMENTAL FACTORS

Dangerous men

Brandon *et al.* (2008) found that men, normally the child's father or partner of the child's mother, were often implicated as abusers but it was not always possible to establish who the perpetrators were without confessions. Males, especially mother's partners and male care workers, are over-represented in the cases in Scotland (see Table 4.1). There was a male perpetrator in all of the key cases, though women were implicated in a number of cases as well, for example, Carla Nicole Bone's mother was convicted of culpable homicide and Danielle Reid's mother was convicted of perverting the course of justice. In Kerelaw both male and female workers were reported to the Procurator Fiscal but only male workers were convicted.

Although men may be more likely to kill or abuse children than women, safe care and parenting programmes tend to be directed primarily at mothers. Schnitzer and Ewigman (2005) point out that educational campaigns around shaken babies are aimed mostly at mothers even though it is fathers or mother's partners who are most likely to shake babies.

Table 4.1 The perpetrator of child death and significant abuse cases in Scotland

Case	Perpetrator/suspected perpetrator
Richard Clark	Family friends
Kennedy McFarlane	Mother's partner
Caleb Ness	Mother's partner
Carla Nicole Bone	Mother's partner
Danielle Reid	Mother's partner
Orkney	Parents and family friends
Eilean Siar	Parents and family friends
Colyn Evans	Male stranger
Dunblane	Male stranger
Edinburgh	Male care workers
Fife	Male care workers
Historical Abuse Systemic Review	Care workers
Kerelaw	Male care workers

The theme of dangerous men has been identified in a number of inquiries into abuse in residential care. A 'macho' culture was identified as a contributory factor to abuse in the three inquiries examined by Berridge and Brodie (1996). The Kerelaw Inquiry commented that the macho culture at Kerelaw Residential School and Secure Unit with its emphasis on control and authority was an important contributory factor to the abuse that young people suffered. Wolmar (cited in Colton, 2002) comments that the increase in the number of male staff in residential homes after the 1960s has been a major factor in abuse in residential child care. He argued that while male staff offered useful role models, greater safeguards should be put in place when they were employed. Pringle (1993) went so far as to question the role of men in care services at all.

Age of parents/carers

There is some evidence to suggest that children of young parents might be at more risk of being killed or seriously abused (Sidebotham *et al.*, 2008). Other studies have, however, been less conclusive.

Findings from England and Wales

- In the Owers *et al.* (1999) study the average age of the mother at the time of the child's birth was 22; only 1 of the 10 mothers was over 30; 4 were under 20.
- The age of mothers was not always known in the Brandon *et al.* (2002) study but 4 out of 10 mothers were known to be over 30; just 2 mothers were under 20 at the time of the child's birth.
- Parents' date of birth was not always included in the 47 cases analysed by Brandon *et al.* (2008) but from the information that was available many mothers and fathers were older; 17 mothers were under 21.

📑 9 of the 40 main carers (23%) in the Sinclair and Bullock (2002) study were under 21 when their child was born.

The age of most of the parents and their partners was missing in the Scottish inquiry and review reports but where information was available parents and carers tended to be older. Richard Clark's parents were over 30, as were the parents of Caleb Ness and the parents of the children in Eilean Siar. Danielle Reid's mother was 24 and the authors of the Kennedy McFarlane report commented that Kennedy's mother was young when she started her family.

Financial problems

High rates of dependence on welfare benefits and/or financial problems have been found in households where children die or suffer serious abuse (Sanders *et al.*, 1999; Wilczynski, 1995; Sinclair and Bullock, 2002). A third of families in the Brandon *et al.* (2008) study were living in poverty (poor living conditions were used as a proxy for poverty) but this is likely to be a significant underestimate since poverty was rarely recorded. A very high level of poverty and deprivation was also a feature of the Brandon *et al.* (2002) study, with evidence of material problems in nine out of 10 families.

Presumably because agencies are not primarily concerned with improving the socio-economic circumstances of families, inquiry and review reports often include only minimal information on families' financial positions. Evidence of financial problems could, however, be discerned in several of the Scottish inquiry and review reports:

- Richard Clark's family suffered financial difficulties and first came to the notice of the social work department as a result of their rent arrears. The family friends who looked after Richard also had financial difficulties.

- The family in Eilean Siar received financial help and advice on managing their debts when they lived in England.

- Members of Danielle Reid's mother's family revealed she was not well off and had rent arrears. They bought her buggies and prams to help out which she later sold.

- Thomas Hamilton, the man who killed 16 children and their teacher at Dunblane Primary school, was in serious financial difficulties, particularly in the last six months of his life. He had been registered as unemployed for many years but had lost his right to claim unemployment benefit when it was found he had been trading in cameras. He ran a number of boys clubs and charged parents a small fee but regularly made a financial loss.

There was little evidence in the inquiry and review reports to suggest that agencies had attempted to analyse the potential implications of families' financial problems.

CASE

Carla Nicole Bone's family made repeated requests for money from the social work department when they were short of food or fuel and received money for milk and gas to heat their caravan on numerous occasions. The authors of the review report into Carla's death state, however, that:

> We did not find reference to why there was never enough money or what Carla's father was contributing to the family budget. There was nothing noted about why this was happening or where the available money was going ... Poverty and struggling to provide for a young child is implicated in adding extra stress and attention to the root causes of poverty in Carla's family and could have been usefully explored.

Practice implications

On its own poverty is unlikely to be a predictor of child death or significant abuse but Brandon *et al.* (2002) comment that poverty may form a backdrop to other factors which are known to be likely to impede parents' capacity to protect their children. Professionals should, therefore, consider the implications of poverty and financial problems in families where parenting problems have already been identified.

Housing

Housing difficulties have been found to be common in families where children die or are seriously abused and victims' families tend to move home more frequently than other families (Sanders *et al.*, 1999; Wilczynski, 1995).

Findings from England and Wales

- In Brandon et al.'s (2008) sample of 47 cases there was evidence of house moves for a third of parents or carers; a similar proportion were living in poor conditions.
- Sinclair and Bullock (2002) found evidence of poverty or accommodation problems in 17 out of 40 cases and in 19 cases the families had moved frequently.
- 4 in 10 families had frequently changed address in both the Owers et al. (1999) and the Brandon et al. (2002) studies.

Housing was particularly significant in the Victoria Climbie case. The first contact that Victoria and her great aunt had with any agency in the UK was with the Homeless Persons' Unit. One of Lord Laming's criticisms of social workers who were involved in the Victoria Climbie case was that they 'failed to address Victoria's needs as an individual and instead treated her as part of ... Kouao's homelessness case'. (Laming, 2003)

Duty staff in the social work teams that dealt with Victoria's case were overwhelmed by referrals from homeless people arriving from overseas and it was estimated that they spent 80% of their time working on housing and homelessness issues. The problem of tracking children at risk of harm who live in families who move frequently was raised in the Inquiry report into Victoria's death and the recommendations in the report led to the government's proposals for the information sharing system 'ContactPoint'.

Housing was a significant issue in a number of the Scottish inquiry and review reports. Families moving around and agencies not being able to establish contact with them was a recurring theme. Several of the families moved address frequently and a number of families had previously lived in England:

- All the families involved in the Orkney Inquiry had previously lived in England.
- Caleb Ness's mother had previously lived in England and her second child had been born there.
- The family in Eilean Siar moved from England in 1995 and there were suggestions they may have moved there to escape the high level of surveillance they had received from agencies in England.
- Danielle Reid and her family moved nine times in five years, between three local authorities.
- Colyn Evans was born in South Wales; his family moved to Fife when he was four; he lived at home until he was 15 when he went to live at Geilsland School; after leaving Geilsland at 17 he returned home but was allocated a single flat a few months later when his home situation deteriorated; two months later he went to Wales for a short period of time before returning to Fife.

CASE

The Caleb Ness case illustrates the important role that housing agencies can play in protecting children. Caleb's mother, Shirley, lived with Caleb in a small, cramped flat and one of her bedrooms was damp. After leaving prison her partner, Alexander Ness, lived with his elderly mother. He then borrowed a flat from a friend for three months and had a succession of temporary addresses until he was hospitalised. Following his discharge from hospital with brain injury he went to live with Shirley who was by then pregnant with Caleb. Shirley and Alexander initially applied to the Housing Department as a couple but their relationship broke down before Caleb's birth and Alexander went to stay with his sister and made an individual application for housing. He was eventually given a bed at a hotel as a single homeless person. Despite having a brain injury he was never assessed as needing supported accommodation, partly because his criminal justice social worker had never asked for medical advice about the extent and implications of his injury. The authors of the inquiry report into Caleb's death expressed concern that such a vulnerable adult was not provided with his own tenancy and went so far as to state that 'It is thought provoking to realise that if supported accommodation had been available for Ness, Caleb's death might not have happened'.

While critical of the fact that Alexander Ness was not provided with appropriate housing and support, they accepted that it would have been difficult to keep track of him as he moved from one place to another, because access to support is often dependent upon someone having an address where they can be contacted.

Practice implications

Housing may be the first agency to have contact with a child. Housing workers should, therefore, be alert to signs of abuse and neglect and know what to do if they have concerns about a child.

CASE

The accommodation in which Carla Nicole Bone's family lived was not ideal for a young baby. Carla was born in England and moved many times in her life:

Carla's mother moved back to Aberdeen with Carla when she was three weeks old and she and Carla moved in with Carla's father and his parents.

When Carla was two months old she and her mother moved from the paternal grandparents' home into a caravan, followed by homeless accommodation, then a woman's refuge.

When Carla was three months old she and her mother moved into a caravan with Carla's father.

The relationship between Carla's mother and father broke down when Carla was nine months old and Carla and her mother moved into a caravan with a man who later became Carla's mother's partner.

When Carla was a year old she, her mother and her mother's partner moved to Aberdeenshire.

> After moving to Aberdeenshire Carla's family requested that all future visits from social workers or health visitors be pre-arranged. With the wisdom of hindsight the authors of the review report comment that this was: '...strange as in the past visits had always been welcomed. A high number of missed appointments and home visits where the workers got no reply or the family failed to turn up at a clinic can be significant'.
>
> **Practice implications**
>
> Families moving home frequently and/or no longer welcoming visits may be indicators that something is wrong.

Criminal behaviour

Child killers or perpetrators of significant abuse have frequently been found to have criminal records, with a high proportion having convictions for violent crimes (Sanders *et al.*, 1999; Wilczynski, 1995; Brandon *et al.*, 2005).

Findings from England and Wales

- More than half of the parents/carers in the cases reviewed by Brandon *et al.* (2008) had a criminal record.
- 6 (15%) primary carers had a criminal record in the Sinclair and Bullock (2002) study and 14 (35%) secondary carers.
- In the Owers and Brandon study (1999) 9 out of 10 parents or caregivers had criminal convictions.
- In the Brandon *et al.* (2002) study 6 out of 10 parents or secondary carers had a criminal record.
- Parental criminality was a feature in 5 of the 12 reviews analysed by Morris *et al.* (2007).

Many of the adults in the inquiry and review reports in Scotland had criminal convictions and police intelligence suggested that some of those who did not have criminal convictions had been involved in criminal activity:

- The couple who abused Richard Clark had been found guilty of neglecting their own children – David Duncan had been imprisoned for three months and Jean Duncan had been placed on probation for two years. Richard's mother was placed on probation for two years after pleading guilty to breaking into her gas meter; she was also charged with attempted murder after stabbing Richard's father in front of her children.
- The father of the children in Eilean Siar was a Schedule 1 offender who had been convicted of indecent assault of his nine-year-old daughter from a previous marriage.
- The man who killed Caleb Ness served most of a five-year sentence for

drug-related offences. His criminal history included a conviction for very serious assault of an adult. Caleb's mother had a long history of convictions relating to prostitution, theft, shoplifting, fraud and breach of the peace. She had been on probation many times and had served at least two prison sentences.

- Police had records containing intelligence pertaining to the violent past history of the man who killed Danielle Reid. The records contained allegations of violent threats towards women and children. Lee Gaytor had a long list of previous convictions for assault, bail offences, theft, breach of the peace and misuse of drugs. The police also had records on Danielle's mother which referred to her supplying drugs to a prisoner.

- Colyn Evans had a long offending history which began at the age of 12 and included charges for shameless indecency, lewd and libidinous behaviour, breach of the peace, breaking into a car and stealing a bike

- Thomas Hamilton did not have a criminal record but the police had received many complaints about him relating to physical assault, neglect and photographing of boys, and he had been questioned on numerous occasions.

The police and criminal justice agencies may hold crucial information about adults that professionals working with children need to know about in order to protect them.

Mental illness

A high prevalence of mental illness has been found among adults in the families of children who are victims of death or significant abuse (Falkov, 1996; Sanders *et al.*, 1999; Sidebotham, 2001; Reder and Duncan, 1999; Wilczynski, 1995).

Findings from England and Wales

- There was evidence of parental mental ill health in 55% of cases reviewed by Brandon *et al.* (2008).

- 18 of the 40 (45%) mothers in the Sinclair and Bullock (2002) study had mental health problems, mostly depression; 9 secondary carers had mental health problems.

- Mental health problems featured in 2 of the 10 cases reviewed by Owers *et al.* (1999) and 6 of the 10 cases reviewed by Brandon *et al.* (2002).

- Emotional/mental health issues were a feature in half the reviews analysed by Morris *et al.* (2007).

- Mental illness featured in 14 (28%) of the case reviews evaluated by Ofsted (2008a).

There was a high prevalence of psychiatric illness, mostly depression, in the cases in Scotland:

- Richard Clark's mother suffered from depression. She received residential treatment at a psychiatric hospital for one year as a condition of her probation order after she stabbed her husband.

- The mother of the children in Eilean Siar received support from mental health services for depression.

- The man who killed Caleb Ness suffered from depression. Caleb's mother also suffered from post-natal depression after Caleb was born.

- Concerns about Kennedy McFarlane's mother's health were raised at the trial. Prior to Kennedy's death a GP raised the possibility that her mother might be suffering from Munchausen syndrome by proxy.

- Despite suspicions that Thomas Hamilton was mentally ill, expert witnesses concluded that he did not and never had suffered from a mental illness but may have had a personality disorder which manifested itself in paranoia and a desire to control others.

While many parents with mental health problems will be able to parent quite effectively, mental health issues should be taken into account when assessing parenting capacity. Ofsted (2008a) found that mental health was not always appropriately considered as part of assessing risk of harm to children, and Brandon *et al.* (2002) found examples of an unrealistic view of parenting capacity in relation to mental health in the cases they reviewed. Reder *et al.* (2001) have argued that there is a need for a change in professionals' mindset towards an understanding that the child is at risk from their parents' *behaviour* rather than from their mental health *diagnosis.*

Substance misuse

A high prevalence of alcohol or drug misuse has been found among the adults in the families of children who suffer significant abuse (Reder *et al.*, 1993; Wilczynski, 1995; Cleaver *et al.*, 2007).

Findings from England and Wales

- Substance misuse was associated with 57% of the cases reviewed by Brandon *et al.* (2008).

- Concerns about drug and alcohol misuse were identified in a third of the reviews evaluated by Ofsted (2008a); in 5 cases a baby was found dead after sleeping with a parent and in all of these cases there was evidence of suspected alcohol/substance misuse by the parent sleeping with the baby.

- 14 of the 40 primary carers and 15 of the secondary carers abused alcohol and/or drugs in the Sinclair and Bullock (2002) study.

▣ Parental drug and alcohol problems were identified in 2 of the 12 reviews analysed by Morris *et al.* (2007).

▣ Drug or alcohol abuse featured in 4 of the 10 cases analysed by Owers *et al.* (1999) and 8 out of 10 cases analysed by Brandon *et al.* (2002).

There was a similarly high prevalence of substance misuse in the cases in Scotland:

- Richard Clark's mother had a drink problem and on one occasion took an overdose of sleeping tablets.

- The man who killed Caleb Ness had a history of heavy drinking and took illicit drugs. Caleb's mother had been a drug addict for more than 20 years and took methadone by prescription throughout her pregnancy. There were a number of references to her drinking alcohol and she had been warned by a doctor of the dangers of combining alcohol with methadone.

- Concerns about Kennedy McFarlane's mother's use of medication, including possible illegal drugs, were raised at the trial. Toxicology reports showed that Kennedy had diazepam in her blood and ibuprofen in her stomach at the time of death.

- Referrals to social work services in relation to Danielle Reid included concerns about her mother's drinking and drug use and her mother's partner's drug use.

- One of the abusers in the Edinburgh Inquiry was reported by other staff for drinking while on duty; a social work department investigation identified problems associated with his use of alcohol.

- Colyn Evans was found in possession of cannabis while at residential school.

If someone misuses substances it may impact upon his or her capacity to parent. There is a considerable body of research to show that children who grow up in substance-misusing families are at increased risk of harm (Barnard, 2007; Cleaver *et al.*, 1999; Kroll and Taylor, 2003).

> It is important to acknowledge that the ability to provide a safe and nurturing environment for children does not have to be compromised by parental substance misuse and many parents who misuse substances are able to provide 'good enough parenting' for their children. (Craig, 2009, p. 121)

It will, however, be necessary to consider the impact of substance misuse in assessing parenting capacity and families may need considerable levels of support from both child and adult services if we are to ensure that children living in substance-misusing families are safe.

Disability

Research studies have found that a significant number of adults in families where children suffer significant abuse have learning difficulties (Reder *et al.*, 1993; Brandon *et al.*, 2005).

Findings from England and Wales

- 11% of parents/carers were reported to have a learning disability in the Brandon *et al.* (2008) study.
- Ofsted (2008a) found that learning difficulties and/or disabilities were often linked with mental health issues for parents and children.
- 3 secondary carers had a learning disability in the 40 cases analysed by Sinclair and Bullock (2002).
- Parental learning disability was apparent in 2 out of 10 cases reviewed by Brandon *et al.* (2002).

Some of the adults in the families in the Scottish inquiry and review reports had a disability or learning difficulty:

- The mother in Eilean Siar had attended a special school and described herself as having a learning disability; she also had epilepsy.
- Danielle Reid's mother was registered blind; she suffered from an inherited neuro-degenerative condition characterised by spastic paraplegia, low IQ, dementia and optic atrophy.
- The man who killed Caleb Ness had a brain injury.

These adults' disabilities undoubtedly contributed in some way to the death or serious abuse of the child. Caleb Ness's death was directly linked to Alexander Ness's brain injury. At trial Alexander Ness plead guilty to culpable homicide on the grounds of diminished responsibility caused by his brain injury. The authors of the inquiry report concluded that his disability was so serious that he should never have had unsupervised care of Caleb. Danielle Reid's mother did not kill Danielle and the mother of the children in Eilean Siar did not abuse her children but disability probably played an indirect role in the death or abuse of the children because it meant these mothers were more vulnerable and less able to protect their children than other mothers.

Parents with learning disabilities or other disabilities should have an equal opportunity to raise their children but the fact that they are as likely, or as unlikely, to harm their children as any other parent should be borne in mind

(Jakob and Gumbrell, 2009). Parents with disabilities may not be able to parent without support, and disability may affect a parent or carer's capacity to understand the needs of their child and ensure they are adequately cared for and protected (Brandon *et al.*, 2002). Disability is, therefore, an important factor to take into account when assessing a family's need for services.

Domestic abuse

Domestic abuse is an important indicator of child maltreatment. Adults in households in which children die or suffer significant abuse have frequently been found to have relationship problems, and domestic abuse has been a common feature (Sanders *et al.*, 1999; Reder *et al.*, 1993; Wilczynski, 1995; Department of Health, 1991a; Brandon *et al.*, 2005; Cleaver *et al.*, 2007).

Findings from England and Wales

- Domestic violence featured in two-thirds of the cases reviewed by Brandon *et al.* (2008).
- Concerns about domestic violence featured in 15 (30%) of the reviews evaluated by Ofsted (2008a); domestic violence was linked to drug and alcohol concerns in 8 of these cases.
- Domestic violence featured in 5 of the 12 reviews analysed by Morris *et al.* (2007).
- 22 of the 31 current partners (71%) of mothers in the Sinclair and Bullock (2002) study were known to be violent; 12 relationships were marked by chronic and serious violence and another 13 by intermittent outbursts.
- Domestic violence featured in a third of the cases reviewed by Owers *et al.* (1999) and 7 out of 10 of the cases analysed by Brandon *et al.* (2002).

Rather surprisingly, domestic abuse can be identified as a factor in only one of the key cases in Scotland – the Richard Clark Inquiry where the perpetrator of the abuse was actually Richard's mother and the victim his father. Richard and his brother witnessed their mother stab their father. Carla Nicole Bone's mother lived in a women's refuge for a short time while she was in a relationship with Carla's father but there was no evidence presented in the review report to suggest that Carla's mother's relationship with the man who killed Carla was violent. The man who killed Danielle Reid was known to police for alleged violence towards his ex-partner, with whom he had a child, but no evidence was presented in the review report to suggest that he had been violent to Danielle's mother.

There was, however, some evidence of friction in the relationships between the adults in some of the cases in Scotland. There were strains in the relationship between Caleb Ness's mother and her partner when they lived together before Caleb's birth, due to Alexander's high level of dependence on Shirley following his brain injury. Shirley eventually asked Alexander to leave and they were living apart by the time Caleb was born. The authors of the inquiry report suggested that Shirley may have been afraid of Alexander. The authors of the Eilean Siar report similarly suggested that the children's mother may have been afraid of and intimidated by her husband. While the inquiry and review reports provide no evidence of domestic abuse towards women there are, therefore, intimations of violence. Many of the children's mothers were particularly vulnerable and some of the men they were living with were certainly known to have been violent to other adults and/or children.

Although many mothers who live with domestic abuse are able to provide adequate care and protection for their children, domestic abuse can make parenting more difficult (Radford and Hester, 2006). Children and young people who are affected by domestic abuse may require substantial levels of support and protection.

> Ensuring individual children and young people receive the most appropriate, effective and timely response, however, remains a complex task. Some children affected by domestic abuse will be in need of protection and will require immediate and sometimes long-term statutory child-care involvement. Others will require a package of support as 'children in need'. (Peckover, 2009)

Owers *et al.* (1999) point out that a culture of violence can become the norm for both workers and families resulting in the impact of violence not always being given sufficient attention. It is important, therefore, that professionals remain always alert to the possibility of domestic abuse.

History of abuse/care

Adults who kill or abuse children, or who live in households where children die or suffer serious abuse, have sometimes been found to have been in care themselves, or to have been abused or separated from their parents (Reder and Duncan, 1999; Reder *et al.*, 1993; Wilczynski, 1995). In contrast to other researchers Sidebotham (2001) did not find that parental history of childhood abuse was a strong predictor of subsequent maltreatment.

Findings from England and Wales

- In the Sinclair and Bullock (2002) study a fifth of primary carers had been in care as children; 15% were known to have been abused when young and in another case abuse was implied. 10% of secondary carers had a history of being in care and 8% came from abusive backgrounds.
- Owers *et al.* (1999) found evidence of intergenerational abuse in a third of cases.
- Brandon *et al.* (2002) found evidence of intergenerational abuse in 70% of cases, and 40% of mothers and 10% of fathers had been in care.

Brandon *et al.* (2002) commented that a major weakness of the cases they analysed was that very little information was collected or made available about the children's parents, including their own childhood histories. Such information is useful because it gives practitioners important insights into parents' states of mind and their ability to care for and protect their children. There was limited information about the past histories of parents and other adults in the Scottish inquiry and review reports. There was, however, evidence that the mother of the children in Eilean Siar had been sexually and physically abused by her father, that both Carla Nicole Bone's parents had been in care, that Kennedy McFarlane's father had been brought up by his grandmother and that Thomas Hamilton was adopted by his grandparents and grew up believing his mother was his sister.

The authors of the Carla Nicole Bone report comment that they were unable to find much information about the childhood experiences of Carla's birth parents in files.

> It would have been valuable to have obtained as full information from their childhood experiences as possible to help to plan how to support this young family with a very new baby. Seeking comprehensive information from the area where the parents of Carla had been looked after would have highlighted the vulnerability of Carla's mother and her apparently poor parenting experiences. (NESCPC, 2003)

Experiences of sexual abuse and/or family violence are known to feature frequently in the backgrounds of young people displaying sexually problematic behaviour and this was a feature in the Colyn Evans case. Colyn was assaulted by his father when he was 13, resulting in his father receiving a warning from the Child Protection Unit (CPU). When he was 15 Colyn was reported missing and found three days later having been with an older man who he later alleged sexually assaulted him.

Most parents who have been abused or spent time in care go on to do a perfectly adequate job of bringing up children themselves but the evidence from inquiries and reviews suggests that professionals should be alert to the fact that adults' childhood experiences may impact on their own parenting abilities.

Previous maltreatment

Child deaths or significant abuse incidents are rarely one-off episodes. Where children die or suffer significant abuse a pattern of prior maltreatment can usually be identified. Previous history of maltreatment is important in assessing vulnerability to recurrence of harm (Jones *et al.*, 2006). A history of neglect and emotional abuse as well as physical abuse has frequently been found but sexual abuse is normally far less prevalent (Reder *et al.*, 1993; Wilczynski, 1995).

Findings from England and Wales

- In over half of the cases reviewed by Brandon *et al.* (2008) there was recorded evidence of prior concerns or a history of abuse and neglect; in the remaining cases the incident appeared to have been a one-off event which came without prior warning.

- In the Sinclair and Bullock (2002) study three-quarters of cases were isolated events; less than a quarter followed a history or pattern of abuse or neglect.

- History of abuse or neglect was a feature in 5 out of 12 of the cases in the Morris *et al.* (2007) study.

- In all but 2 of the 10 cases reviewed by Owers *et al.* (1999) there was a history of previous injuries and a pattern of previous admissions to hospital; there were 4 previous deaths of a child in the families concerned

- In the Brandon *et al.* 2002 study there was a history of injuries and/or previous hospital admissions in half of the 10 cases and 3 previous child deaths in the families.

The Victoria Climbie report identified a long pattern of previous maltreatment towards Victoria. A social worker had been involved with Victoria in France following the issuing of a Child at Risk Emergency Notification by Victoria's school. Once Victoria arrived in England there were numerous investigations of suspected non-accidental injury as well as concerns about emotional abuse and neglect. Victoria's great-aunt also alleged on one occasion that Victoria had been sexually abused by her partner and Victoria initially corroborated the story.

Neglect has been identified as an important theme in the more recent analyses of Serious Case Reviews in England and Wales. Owers *et al.* (1999) have pointed out that it is particularly difficult to predict neglect cases because the families involved in these cases differ little from many other families that agencies work with. Despite poor home conditions professionals often comment that the children in families where neglect is a feature are happy. 'There are different professional perceptions and judgements of what is an acceptable level of emotional poverty within the context of appalling material hardship' (Owers, p. 40).

There was frequently a history of physical and emotional abuse, as well as neglect, in the cases in Scotland and sexual abuse sometimes featured too. In a number of cases perpetrators had previously abused and/or neglected other children:

- Richard Clark and his brother were neglected by their own parents and taken into care for two months in 1972. The family friends who were later found guilty of assaulting Richard had been found guilty of neglecting their own daughters in 1969; their daughters were placed with foster parents but were later returned home.

- Caleb Ness's mother had two older children taken into permanent care as a result of neglect and failure to end her drug addiction.

- Kennedy McFarlane's GP and playgroup expressed a number of concerns about Kennedy's hair falling out, soiling and decline in her general well-being; non-accidental injury had been suspected on numerous occasions when she suffered sore eyes, back pain and bruising to her face.

- There were concerns about the poor quality of the accommodation in which Carla Nicole Bone lived and poor levels of cleanliness; there were also many references to Carla's poor weight gain. It emerged at the trial that the level of force used in feeding Carla was violent and after her death her mother spoke of hitting her. Odd bruises had been noted on visits but there was no evidence at the time to indicate she was being abused.

- Thomas Hamilton was never charged with any offence relating to abuse against a child but his previous conduct showed indications of paedophilia. He ran various boys clubs over a twenty-year period and parents and helpers frequently expressed concern that his methods of running the clubs were over regimented, even militaristic. He was alleged to have physically abused boys on more than one occasion. He showed an unusual interest in individual boys, insisted that for gymnastics the boys wear black swimming trunks and often videoed and took photographs of the boys posing in their trunks. Concerns about him as far back as 1974 had led to his name being entered on a Scout 'blacklist' intended to ensure unsuitable candidates were denied appointment.

- Colyn Evans had a history of harmful sexual behaviour and had been sexually abusive towards adults and children on a number of previous occasions before he killed Karen Dewar.

CASE

The Eilean Siar case involved issues of physical, sexual and emotional abuse and neglect over a long period of time, spanning generations. The father of the three children who were the subject of the review report was a Schedule 1 offender who had assaulted his nine-year-old daughter from a previous marriage. As a result the three children had been on the Child Protection Register for sexual abuse almost continuously; they had also been registered for physical abuse and physical neglect. Between 1990 and 2001 professionals recorded 222 child protection-related concerns about the children. There were:

29 records of suspected non-accidental injury and allegations of sexual abuse;

22 records of incidents which SWIA describe as neglect;

171 recorded instances where the children had marks, bruises or other physical injuries, or where there were concerns about their health, including genital soreness, wetting, soiling and worries about their development.

When the evidence is presented in this way it appears incredible that professionals did not decide to take the children into care earlier.

Practice implications

Practitioners need to look at patterns of abuse and neglect and not just respond to isolated incidents

Prior contact with agencies

Child deaths and significant abuse might be expected to occur more frequently in families where there is little contact with statutory services and little opportunity for monitoring children's safety. Previous research has found, however, that far from being hidden away from contact, victims and their families are often seen by a range of agencies in the time leading up to the death or significant abuse. While some families are hostile towards statutory agencies and shut out professionals, fail to keep appointments or disappear from view, others have been viewed as cooperative and willing to receive help.

In a number of cases in the Brandon et al. (2002) study, professionals visiting families experienced intimidation from fathers. There were also examples of parents not keeping appointments and not allowing children to have medical assessments or treatments. The intimidation of parents sometimes inhibited professionals or caused them not to act. In one of the cases analysed by Owers et al. (1999) two children were removed from the register because staff could not gain cooperation from parents: 'The agency's acceptance of the family's refusal to co-operate signalled the end of involvement rather than acting as a trigger for a multi-agency assessment' (p. 34).

Victoria Climbie had little contact with statutory agencies in the weeks leading up to her death and it appears there may have been attempts to conceal her from public view in the last weeks of her life. She did, however, have a significant amount of contact with a number of agencies prior to that. She did not attend school and was not always registered with a GP but had numerous contacts with social services, health and the police.

Findings from England and Wales

- 6 out of 40 children in the Sinclair and Bullock (2002) study were on the Child Protection Register; 12 cases were defined as children in need; for 16 children no concerns about their welfare had ever been expressed; in 12 cases children were unknown to social services departments at the time of the incident but 13 had been known for more than 3 years; social services involvement was generally low and less than that of health professionals; nearly half of families were seen as cooperative and responsible.

- 12% of children in the Brandon *et al.* (2008) study were on the Child Protection Register and 55% known to social care; in some cases children had been referred to children's social care but had not met the threshold for intervention; in others the parent would not accept offers of help; at the time of the incident almost half of the children were known only to universal services but 83% had been known to children's social care at some point; a number of cases had been closed days or weeks before the incident; in many cases families were known to adult services.

- 18% of children in the Rose and Barnes (2008) study had their names on the register.

- 35 out of 50 children (70%) in the Ofsted (2008a) evaluation were known to social services; all children were known to universal services; 13 of the 50 were on the register at the time of the incident; the younger the child the less likely they were to be on the register.

- Failure to attend appointments was a feature in 4 of the 10 cases reviewed by Owers *et al.* (1999); in at least 4 out of 10 cases there was a history of poor school attendance.

- Failure to attend appointments was a feature in 9 out of 10 cases reviewed by Brandon *et al.* (2002); aggressiveness towards professionals was a feature in 4 cases.

- In the Ofsted (2008a) evaluation families not keeping appointments was a feature in 5 cases of young babies and in 3 families where there was chronic neglect.

- Ofsted (2008a) found that missed appointments were recorded but no-one questioned their significance; there were examples of children being off school for considerable periods of time without any follow up; an issue in one review was lack of oversight of children receiving home education; some families had an unusually large number of appointments with health services.

Most of the children and young people or families involved in the cases in Scotland had had contact with a number of agencies, including social work, but levels of contact varied considerably. Only Caleb Ness and the children in Eilean Siar were on the Child Protection Register. Richard Clark would probably have been on the Child Protection Register if such a register had existed back in 1975. He did receive compulsory measures of supervision from a Children's Hearing as did the children in Eilean Siar.

The family in Eilean Siar received an astounding level of support from social work, health, education and the voluntary sector. SWIA found that almost 100 different professionals had had contact with the children in England and Eilean Siar: 29 child protection case conferences were held in respect of the children, 21 statutory reviews were convened after they became looked after, and the Reporter arranged 24 Children's Hearings. In addition the children's mother received mental health support in England and the family received support from criminal justice, community care, NCH, psychiatry, and educational psychology in Eilean Siar.

CASE

Danielle Reid had been flagged as a child with special needs following her birth in Aberdeen. She was placed on the 'special observation register' by Grampian NHS and offered annual appointments to monitor her progress due to the risk of her developing her mother's neuro-degenerative condition. Danielle was, however, not adequately monitored by the NHS because her mother moved frequently. She attended nursery and started school but after two months her mother informed the school that she was leaving to live in Manchester. This was the last time she was seen by any agency. She was, however, not killed until some weeks later and it is possible she was deliberately hidden away.

Danielle had less prior contact with agencies than the other children who died or were significantly injured in their own homes in Scotland. Two referrals were made to social work relating to concerns about Danielle but both resulted in no further action. It was not until a family member reported Danielle missing that the police became involved and a referral was made to the Reporter. By this time Danielle was already dead. The author of the Danielle Reid report pointed out that if children are removed from health and education services, this takes away the only existing professional scrutiny of their welfare. Danielle was not on a school register at the time of her death and there was no way to track her once she was removed from the school roll. Like Victoria Climbie she effectively vanished from view in the weeks before her death. The report into Danielle's death recommended that systems be put in place to ensure adequate tracking of vulnerable children and possibly tracking of parents as well.

Practice implications

Poor attendance at school may be an indicator of child protection issues and should always be investigated.

CASE

Colyn Evans had a lot of contact with various agencies.

He was first referred to social work at age 12 for difficult behaviour, truancy and being outwith parental control. A referral was made to the Reporter but no further formal action was taken as support was already provided at school and by clinical psychology on a voluntary basis.

Two years later the Fife Sex Offender Registrar was notified of concerns about Colyn after he was charged with lewd and libidinous behaviour towards two girls. A Children's Hearing imposed a home supervision requirement and he was referred to a service to address his problematic sexual behaviour. He was entered on the Sex Offender Nominal Record and categorised as a non-registered sex offender. The supervision requirement was terminated the following year as Colyn and his family were willing to accept services on a voluntary basis.

Three months later Colyn was charged with shameless indecency against an adult female and referred again to the Reporter. The incident was not recorded on the Sex offender Nominal Record.

The following month there was a complaint to the police of a physical assault on an eight-year-old boy and a report was sent to the Reporter.

Later the same month Colyn was charged with shameless indecency and there was a further referral to the Reporter. Before the Children's Hearing was held Colyn became a resident at a residential school which provided specialist support to young people with concerning sexual behaviour, initially on a voluntary basis, and then subject to place of safety warrants under a supervision requirement by a Children's Hearing.

Colyn's supervision requirement was terminated after his 16th birthday and he was transferred from the Children and Families team to the Throughcare team. He attended a service to address his sexually problematic behaviour but was unwilling to cooperate and the service ended their involvement with him due to his lack of commitment. He was referred to the housing department and provided with a single person flat following deterioration in his home situation.

Over a five-month period throughcare and housing support made 41 visits to Colyn's flat and contact was made on 20 occasions. Council staff continued to try to locate him up until the murder of Karen Dewar. The police also had contact with Colyn during this time. They were alerted when Colyn threatened to commit suicide; they then made several attempts to locate him without success when he was suspected of breaking into a flat. In the months leading up to the murder of Karen Dewar neither the local authority nor the police were able to contact Colyn. Like the families of Danielle Reid and Victoria Climbie it appears he was 'lying low' and trying to avoid contact with the authorities by this point.

Practice implications

Agencies may need to devise more creative ways of engaging hard-to-reach young people on a voluntary basis once they are over 16.

CASE

Kennedy McFarlane did not have contact with the social work department until shortly before her death when a child protection investigation was initiated. A case conference was called in relation to Kennedy but unfortunately this did not take place before her death. She had a significant amount of contact with health professionals prior to her death. She was taken to her GP on numerous occasions for sore eyes and back pain resulting in referrals to hospital amid possible concerns of non-accidental injury. Two weeks before Kennedy's death her GP expressed concern about the number of contacts she had had with the health centre. He considered Kennedy to be at risk and raised the possibility of Munchausen by proxy. On the day before Kennedy died Kennedy's mother was admitted to hospital with a seizure. Kennedy accompanied her and was seen on the ward.

Practice implications

A high number of health visits may be a warning sign.

LEARNING POINTS

✔ **Children may be at more risk from men than women and safe care and parenting programmes should be aimed at men as well as women.**

✔ **Changes of address may indicate that families are attempting to avoid contact by agencies. Professionals should endeavour to maintain a continuous record when families move and minimise disruptions to service provision following moves.**

✔ **The police may hold important information relating to criminal convictions or suspected criminal activity which should be included in assessing the risks adults pose to children.**

✔ **The effects of depression need to be taken into account when assessing risk towards children.**

✔ **Practitioners should assess the risks posed by drug and alcohol misuse, particularly to very young babies. Parents who drink should be advised not to sleep with babies. The police may hold information in relation to drugs that can be used in assessing the risks to children.**

✔ **Professionals should undertake an adequate assessment of the impact of learning difficulties and health issues on adults' capacity to care for and protect their children.**

✔ **All professionals should be aware of the link between domestic abuse and the risk of harm to children and be alert to the risk that violent males pose to vulnerable women and children. Professionals need to find out who is living in households with children.**

✔ **Practitioners should obtain as much information about parents'/ carers' own childhoods as they can and include this information in assessing their caretaking abilities and ability to protect their children.**

✔ **Historical information, such as other children in care, may be a significant risk factor and must be taken into account in assessing risk and need.**

✔ **Patterns of help seeking may be warning signs of parenting difficulties and abuse, e.g. admissions to A&E, a history of injuries or a history of illness.**

✔ **Neglect should be understood in relation to the history and context of the whole case and any patterns which may signal risk to the child.**

✔ **Changes from cooperation to non-cooperation of families may be significant.**

✔ **Children who are at serious risk of harm may not be found within formal child protection procedures. The most vulnerable children may be those on the margins of the child protection system about whom there are some concerns. This highlights the importance of staff in universal services and adult services being able to identify abuse and neglect.**

✔ **Missed appointments may be a warning sign. If a family fails to accept or take up a service this needs to be taken into account in an assessment and may raise the level of concern so child protection procedures need to be followed.**

MULTIPLE RISK FACTORS

While individual risk factors may be significant there are no clear causal relationships between these factors and child death or serious injury (Brandon *et al.*, 2008). Rather, the evidence suggests that it is more likely to be the co-existence of several risk factors and the way in which these various risk factors interact which is important in terms of predicting child death and significant abuse. There is ample evidence to suggest that the families where children die or suffer significant abuse experience a combination of difficulties. Rose and Barnes (2008) commented that few of the children in their study lived with parents with stable relationships, in settled family households, in adequate housing with sufficient resources or community support to meet their needs. Parents coped with a range of problems including substance misuse, mental ill health, learning disabilities, or domestically volatile or violent relationships. They also had uncertain incomes, debts, unsuitable and overcrowded accommodation, and moved frequently. In a few cases they engaged in criminal behaviour to fund their substance use.

Ofsted (2008a) found that it was not unusual for more than one risk factor – drug and alcohol misuse, domestic abuse, mental illness, learning difficulties – to exist in one family. Brandon *et al.* (2008) similarly found that there was coexistence of the problems of domestic violence, parental mental health and parental substance misuse in a third of families. Where vulnerable parents are faced with multiple stress factors their coping capacities will diminish and they may be at increased risk of failing to provide care and protection for their children and may, therefore, place them in situations of risk and danger (Brandon *et al.*, 2002; Cleaver *et al.*, 2007).

The coexistence of a number of risk factors was common in the Scottish inquiry and review reports that investigated the death or abuse of children in the home. Financial problems, housing problems/families' moving frequently, criminal convictions/suspected criminal activity, mental health/disability/health problems and substance misuse were identified in a high proportion of cases and in many cases three or four, even five, of these risk factors were present (see Table 4.2).

Table 4.2 Multiple risk factors

Report	Financial problems	Housing problems/frequent moves	Criminal convictions/suspected criminal activity	Mental health/disability/health problems	Substance misuse
Richard Clark	X		X	X	X
Orkney		X			
Kennedy McFarlane				X	X
Caleb Ness		X	X	X	X
Carla Nicole Bone	X	X	X		
Eilean Siar	X	X	X	X	
Danielle Reid	X	X	X	X	X

LEARNING POINT

✔ **Children are likely to be at most risk when there is a cumulative interaction of risk factors. Professionals need to look at all the risk factors together. One factor on its own may not be important.**

Identifying and understanding interacting risk and protective factors is a core task in work with children and families. The Assessment Framework that is used by practitioners in England and Wales is based on a developmental ecological model that understands the importance of recognising the presence of multiple risk and protective factors and their possible interactions, and the new My World assessment framework in Scotland (as laid out in the Scottish

Government 2008 Guide to GIRFEC) is also based on an assessment of risk and protective factors. The number of factors that interact or decrease the risk of harm to children are, however, extremely complex and 'the complexity of family circumstances means that even if the "whole picture" of family circumstances had been known, it would not always have been possible to predict an outcome for most of the children' (Brandon *et al.*, 2008, p. 106).

Most cases of serious harm may, therefore, be essentially unpredictable. As Laming himself concluded, 'It is unrealistic to expect that it will ever be possible to eliminate the deliberate harm or death of a child – indeed, no system can achieve this' (2003, para. 17.89).

CONCLUSION

This chapter discussed child, family and environmental themes which have been identified in inquiries and reviews in Scotland and elsewhere in the UK. It suggested that the following children might be more likely to die or suffer serious abuse:

❑ very young children;
❑ children who are the only or youngest child in their family;
❑ children who have previously experienced neglect, physical or emotional abuse;
❑ children with special needs, including health problems or behavioural or learning difficulties and/or children who were born prematurely;
❑ hard-to-help teenagers.

To summarise, family and environmental factors which can be identified are:

❑ The presence of violent men, particularly cohabitees of the natural parent;
❑ Poverty;
❑ Housing problems;
❑ Frequent moves;
❑ Parental conflict and/or domestic abuse;
❑ Mental health problems;
❑ Substance misuse;
❑ Young parents;
❑ Social isolation, poor support networks;
❑ Criminal convictions;
❑ Adults coming from abusive/care backgrounds;

❑ Learning difficulties;

❑ Long term involvement with agencies, including adult services;

❑ High levels of involvement with health;

❑ Withdrawal from contact with the outside world – children stop attending nursery or school; are not taken to appointments; professionals fail to gain access; neighbours no longer see the child.

It is possible but unusual for children to die or be seriously abused when only one or a small number of the factors identified above are present. In most cases one risk factor will not be significant: the families where children die or experience significant abuse normally experience difficulties in combination and it is when there is a cumulative interaction of multiple risk factors that children are likely to be at most risk.

Chapter 5 considers agency factors, or factors related to the practice of professionals, which can be identified in key Scottish inquiries or reviews into child deaths or serious abuse.

CHAPTER 5

Agency factors

Introduction

This chapter discusses the agency factors, or factors related to the practice of professionals, which have been identified in key Scottish inquiries or reviews into child deaths or serious abuse and compares them with the practice factors which have been identified in inquiries and reviews in other parts of the UK. As outlined in Chapter 2, the purpose of inquiry and review into child deaths or serious cases is to examine the role of agencies who were involved in a case up to the point at which the death or serious abuse took place, to establish whether any lessons can be learned and to make recommendations to improve practice. While most inquiries and reviews conclude that the child death or significant abuse being investigated could not have been predicted beforehand, there are nevertheless normally lessons to be learned from a case and a number of key agency themes can be identified.

ASSESSMENT AND DECISION MAKING

Findings from England and Wales

- Brandon et al. (2002) found that factors such as alcohol and drug use and domestic violence were missing in assessment; they also found that health assessments were not always undertaken.

- Ofsted (2008a) found little evidence of assessment to evaluate the quality of attachments between parents and children and poor assessment of the impact of neglect; families were subject to multiple assessments and plans without any clear expectation of what needed to change, how that would be demonstrated and what the consequences of non-cooperation for parents would be.

- Brandon et al. (2008) and Rose and Barnes (2008) found examples of failure to take account of past history.

- Owers et al. (1999) and Brandon et al. (2002) found examples of failure to consider the whole picture and overall pattern.

- Brandon et al. (2002) and Owers et al. (1999) found that decisions were sometimes based on partial information because key professionals did not attend meetings or were given inadequate information

- Sinclair and Bullock (2002) found that there was a lack of information on significant males.

ASSESSMENT

Lord Laming highlighted the importance of assessment in the inquiry report into the death of Victoria Climbie. Victoria spent two weeks in a hospital in Middlesex but she was not given a thorough medical examination while she was there, despite the fact this was a requirement of the hospital's child protection procedures if a child presented with possible non-accidental injury.

Problems around assessment were noted in many of the Scottish inquiry and review reports. There were examples of medical assessments not being undertaken (Richard Clark and Kennedy McFarlane); risk assessments not being undertaken (Orkney, Caleb Ness, Kennedy McFarlane, Colyn Evans); and multi-agency assessments of need not being undertaken (Carla Nicole Bone, Eilean Siar).

Assessment frameworks

Several of the inquiry and review reports commented on the lack of assessment tools or frameworks available to professionals. It is, however, what is done with information, rather than its simple accumulation, that leads to more analytic assessments and safer practice, and assessment tools are of limited value in terms of actually helping professionals make sense of, and attribute meaning to, information. Brandon et al. (2002) comment that professionals will only be able to make sense of isolated facts and incidents if they have a theoretical framework within which to analyse them: 'Without such a framework it is very difficult for professionals to work out how each "dot" of information (with different dots often lodged in different agencies) might be connected so that a coherent picture is drawn' (p. 60).

Reder and Duncan (1999) comment that professionals need to learn to think rather than follow checklists and guidelines. They advocate operating 'socratically' — asking questions, thinking through matters and testing hypotheses against the research evidence.

CASE

The authors of the Colyn Evans review report commented that 'Risk assessment is at very best an imprecise activity'. Appropriate risk assessments of Colyn were undertaken: the Child Support Service (CSS) carried out two Assessment, Intervention and Moving On Project (AIM) assessments that concluded Colyn was at high risk of re-offending, and an Adolescent Sexual Abuser Project (ASAP) assessment, completed while Colyn was at residential school, concluded that he was confused about his sexual preferences, overly sexually preoccupied, had considerable problems managing his anger, tended to endorse the use of violence against females and was more likely than average to see the use of violence as a problem-solving strategy.

Despite the results of these risk assessments the residential school decided not to commence work to address Colyn's inappropriate sexual behaviour because he denied the charge of shameless indecency made against him. The authors of the review report questioned the school's decision to take no further action and not commence work in relation to inappropriate sexual behaviour. They concluded that the local authority's actions raised serious concern with regard to their duty of care and protection of others. While at residential school Colyn absconded on a regular basis and there are several references in the review report to engagement in sexual activity with other boys. On one occasion the school even referred Colyn to the genito-urinary clinic but took no further action in relation to the matter.

The report authors were critical of the fact that risk was assessed but no-one actually managed that risk: 'it is of no value to undertake risk assessments and use terms such as "high risk" without developing a management plan to support, and as far as possible, minimise that risk.'

Practice implication

The findings of risk assessments must follow through into decision making and planning. Risk must be managed as well as assessed.

CASE

A criminal justice social worker conducted a risk assessment of the father in Eilean Siar when the family first moved there and concluded he was at low risk of re-offending. The risk assessment was undertaken by one worker whereas risk assessments are normally undertaken by two social workers. It was also at odds with assessments undertaken in England that found the father to be at high risk of re-offending. The findings of this risk assessment lowered the levels of concern about possible sexual abuse in the family and had a significant impact on decisions made in relation to the case until a second risk assessment was undertaken four years later. The authors of the review report comment that professionals failed to realise that 'even the term low risk means there is still a real risk which needs to be managed'.

The second risk assessment was undertaken by two staff and the father was assessed as at high to medium risk of re-offending. He agreed to leave the family home and, under a supervision requirement from the Children's Hearing, was given only supervised access to the children. The children were, however, still not protected because no-one ensured their father had only supervised access and no-one assessed their mother's ability to protect them.

Practice implication

Risk assessments are only one tool to assess the risk an abuser is likely to present to children. They must form part of a wider assessment of the children's needs for care and protection, together with an assessment of the ability of the non-abusing partner to protect them.

Historical information

A full assessment of need cannot be carried out without a detailed examination of a family's circumstances yet there were examples in the Scottish inquiry and review reports of professionals failing to take historical information into account. Sometimes information was not available and failure to take it into account was understandable. There was, for example, a lack of family detail recorded in the health visitor's documentation in relation to Danielle Reid and previous social work contact with Danielle's mother when she was a teenager had been lost. The authors of the review report into Danielle's death concluded that had this information been available someone checking later might have become aware of Danielle's mother's history of vulnerability and disability. Similarly, subsequent investigation into the Kennedy McFarlane case following Kennedy's death revealed information about her mother's health and drug use which would have been very relevant to risk assessment and planning for Kennedy had it been available at the time.

In other cases historical information had been available but its significance had not been fully appreciated. Failure to take account of historical information was a significant finding of the Caleb Ness Inquiry:

- Caleb's mother Shirley's history of failure to care for her other two children was dismissed by professionals as 'historical', despite the fact she was still misusing drugs and there was no evidence to suggest she had changed significantly.

- In assessing risk to Caleb social workers did not seek information about Alexander Ness's criminal background, even though he was on parole.

- Alexander's disabilities were assessed but medical advice as to whether his disabilities might pose a risk to Caleb was not sought.

- No account was taken of Shirley's offending history.

In Eilean Siar historical information was available and considered but professionals were reluctant to judge the parents because of what had happened in their past. The authors of the review report commented that 'Whilst it is important that professionals do not jump to conclusions, or label adults because of past experiences, they must use their expertise to determine whether these experiences are a strength, or weakness, to their parenting.'

Significant males

The partners of vulnerable mothers have been implicated in many child death and significant abuse cases but lack of information on significant males and failure to assess the risk they pose to children has been a significant finding of inquiry and review reports. As we saw in the previous chapter, all the children in the Scottish inquiry and review reports were killed or abused by males (although females were sometimes implicated as well). These males frequently had criminal convictions or had been involved in violent behaviour which was known to the police. A number of inquiry and review reports revealed, however, that agencies were either not aware of this information, or were aware of it but failed to use it, when assessing the risk these individuals posed to children. For example, nursery staff noted a marked decline in Kennedy McFarlane's care and well-being from the time that her mother's partner joined the household. They alerted social workers to the fact that Kennedy appeared to be scared of him but the risks he posed to Kennedy were never formally assessed. Similarly, the professionals who were involved in the Caleb Ness case knew that Alexander Ness would visit often but they failed to undertake a formal review of the potential risk he posed to Caleb. The inquiry report comments that the police could have contributed important information in relation to Alexander's criminal history if his name had been given to them but they were only ever given Caleb's mother's name.

CASE

Danielle Reid's mother Tracy was particularly vulnerable as a result of her disabilities. The man who killed Danielle Reid was known to police as a violent individual but agencies did not know he was living with Danielle's mother. The review report into the death of Danielle concluded that:

> Dangerous perpetrators prey upon the vulnerable and often the vulnerable do not have the resources nor the appropriate professional agency support to ensure that they remain protected ... If it was established practice in Scotland that Police Intelligence or Police information on violent perpetrators was shared automatically and appropriately with other professionals and agencies in contact with children ... the outcome for Danielle may have been different.

Practice implication

Professionals need to be able to track violent adults who may be a significant danger to children.

Although evidence suggests that fathers and other significant males present a higher level of risk to children than mothers, assessments of parenting skills frequently focus on mothers' skills as opposed to those of fathers and other significant males. In part, this may be because professionals are reluctant to work with men whom they perceive to be violent. Reluctance to work with hostile adults can be very dangerous for children. Brandon et al. (2008) comment that where families are hostile there is evidence that 'Workers often became frozen and this hampered their ability to reflect, make judgements and act clearly, and to follow through with referrals, assessments or plans' (p. 96). Visiting uncooperative, hostile families will be very stressful for professionals. While noting that there should be no expectation that professionals should stay in a situation where they feel physically threatened, Pearson (2009) comments that 'Workers must ask themselves if they, as professional adults, are made to feel intimidated and frightened by a parent's behaviour, what is the experience of a child living with parents who respond in such a way?' (p. 96).

DECISION MAKING

Inadequate assessment can lead to poor decision making. Poor decisions may be made in relation to a case if no-one is in possession of all the evidence or the evidence is not considered as a whole. The inquiry into the death of Victoria Climbie found that many of the poor decisions made in relation to Victoria were made because professionals failed to consider the information that was readily available in her file. No-one, not even Victoria's social worker, ever read the whole of Victoria's file and the social worker's manager did not read the file at all. Had the file been read, Lord Laming concluded that it was unlikely Victoria's case would have been closed because it would have been apparent that very few of the tasks that had been identified at the strategy meeting had ever been completed.

Most of the key inquiry and review reports in Scotland highlight examples of erroneous decision making and in some cases this contributed to failure to protect children and young people. Examples of flawed decisions which were identified were:

- Children being left in unsafe situations because professionals placed them with parents or carers or did not remove them sooner (Richard Clark, Eilean Siar, Caleb Ness).

- Children being removed unnecessarily (Orkney).
- Professionals not making a decision at all or taking no action (Caleb Ness, Edinburgh, Danielle Reid).
- Children not being referred to the Reporter (Kennedy McFarlane, Caleb Ness, Edinburgh, Danielle Reid).
- A supervision requirement being discharged (Colyn Evans).
- Professionals not involving the police (Kennedy McFarlane, Danielle Reid).
- The police making poor decisions (Danielle Reid, Dunblane).

CASE

The authors of the Caleb Ness Inquiry report concluded that the decision to allow Caleb to go home, knowing that Alexander Ness would play a significant part in his care, was flawed. A child protection case conference was held while Caleb was still in hospital. Professionals attending the conference decided to place Caleb on the Child Protection Register for physical neglect and not to refer the case to the Reporter. The report authors concluded that these decisions were flawed because major errors in the case conference process meant that the professionals who attended were not presented with all the information:

there was an absence of information about Alec Ness's head injury;

no information was available in relation to Shirley's other children who were in care;

attendees were not informed that Caleb was suffering from neonatal abstinence syndrome which might make him more difficult to care for than other newborn babies;

the chair had never chaired a case conference before and made major errors.

After the conference the health visitor alerted the social worker to what she saw as increased risk factors in Caleb's life but he did nothing. The authors of the inquiry report comment that it is possible Caleb's life might still have been saved at this stage had the social worker decided to bring forward the case conference review date or hold a meeting of core workers: 'It is the absence of any decision at all at this stage which causes us most concern'.

Practice implications

All of the evidence needs to be presented and considered at case conferences in order for professionals to be able to make appropriate decisions about the care and protection of children.

Levels of risk may change at any time. Risk assessment should, therefore, be an ongoing process rather than a one-off exercise.

The protection of children has been likened to a jigsaw puzzle where each agency holds different pieces of the picture and all the pieces need to be put together correctly to enable effective safeguarding decisions to be made. In a number of key cases in Scotland sections of the jigsaw were either missing or professionals were unable to accurately piece them together. For example, the author of the inquiry report into the death of Kennedy McFarlane commented that if senior staff in health or social work had reviewed all the information available to them it would have been clear that Kennedy's care was inadequate to protect her from significant harm. However, 'No-one put all the pieces of the puzzle together creating a total picture of escalating harm within a context of a family in need. If they had done so I am in no doubt that she could and would have been protected' (Hammond, 2001).

A substantial amount of evidence on the family in Eilean Siar was available in social work, health, education and voluntary agency records but information was considered on an incident-by-incident basis rather than as a whole:

> It was the pattern, the enduring nature and the relationship between the physical health issues, physical injuries, the children's behaviour and the physical neglect which were significant. Had these patterns been analysed on a systematic basis, the evidence of a need to remove the children would have been clear. (SWIA, 2005)

Owers *et al.* (1999) made similar comments in relation to some of the cases they reviewed in Wales:

> In part the 'incident led' history of child protection work has militated against understanding the whole context of the child within the history of the family. Factors which should have triggered priority action were not recognised because seen in isolation they were not alarming. (p. 35)

DISTINCTION BETWEEN CHILD IN NEED/CHILD PROTECTION CASES

Decisions which are made about a case may depend to some extent on whether the case is defined as a child in need or a child protection case. Lord Laming identified the distinction that professionals sometimes make between the two types of case as contributing to the failure to protect Victoria Climbie. At several key points he concluded that Victoria's case was not treated with the urgency it required because professionals viewed it as a child in need rather than a child protection case.

> I also heard evidence that the downgrading of cases to the status of section 17, and afterwards closure, was becoming an attractive option to child care teams struggling to deal with what they perceived to be an ever increasing number of child protection referrals, case conferences and registrations … This approach to the use of sections 17 and 47 can only be described as dangerous. It is at odds with my understanding of the aspirations of the Children Act 1989. These factors were clearly evident in the failure to protect Victoria in the four different local authorities, the two hospitals and the one police force. (Laming, 2003)

The distinction between child protection and children in need cases similarly featured in some of the Scottish inquiry and review reports (Carla Nicole Bone, Kennedy McFarlane). The Carla Nicole Bone case was viewed as a child in need case. Carla's family received a high level of professional input but the support they received was predominantly parenting support for Carla's mother, as opposed to support to meet Carla's needs for care and protection.

Cases which are labelled as child protection may progress in an entirely different way from those labelled as children in need. Witnesses in the Danielle Reid review confirmed that priority was given to child protection cases. The authors of the review report concluded that there was too much differential in service provision to the small number of children on Child Protection Registers and/or Statutory Supervision Orders, in comparison with the large numbers of vulnerable children who never appear on such registers or orders but for whom there are concerns about their welfare. They argued that registration should not be the key to securing services:

> The case does raise the question of whether the existing statutory provisions for children in need are adequate and as to their

relationship with the statutory structure for children in need of care and protection ... I remain disturbed that not enough emphasis is being placed on the vulnerable and at risk child who may well never enter any formalised inter-agency child protection procedure. (Herbison, 2005)

While professionals may treat child protection and children in need cases differently, in reality the two types of case cannot always be neatly distinguished. As Lord Laming commented in the Victoria Climbie Inquiry report, 'child protection does not come labelled as such'. While there may be little difference between child protection and child in need cases it is important to remember that where cases have not been defined as child protection, because they have not met the threshold of significant harm, families do not have to engage and any services which are provided will be optional (Hughes, 2009).

The Colyn Evans case also raised issues in relation to the distinction between statutory and voluntary services. The authors of the review report questioned the decision of the Children's Hearing to terminate Colyn's supervision requirement when he left residential school:

> The emphasis in the Children (Scotland) Act is for voluntary measures where this can be reasonably achieved. Although it seemed Colyn was co-operating to a large extent at this stage, his preparedness to undertake specific offence focussed work on his inappropriate sexual behaviour was untested. (SWIA/HMIC, 2005)

They pointed out that there are no realistic sanctions to support compulsory measures for 16- and 17-year-olds. In theory a supervision requirement can continue until a young person is 18, but in reality the sanctions that can be applied to 16- and 17-year-olds are limited and a Children's Hearing has little capacity to control a young person's behaviour if he or she chooses not to comply with a supervision requirement. It can be difficult for agencies to work with young people like Colyn who refuse to engage on a voluntary basis but the high number of SCRs relating to teenagers in England as outlined in Chapter 4 suggests that there is an urgent need to consider more effective ways of engaging these hard-to-reach young people.

PLANNING

A number of the Scottish inquiry and review reports were critical of professionals for not formulating a plan to protect children and meet their needs

(Colyn Evans, Eilean Siar, Caleb Ness, Carla Nicole Bone, Orkney, Kennedy McFarlane). For children on the register, child protection guidelines state that a child protection plan must be agreed at a case conference. Caleb Ness's name was placed on the Child Protection Register following a case conference but witnesses who were interviewed in the inquiry into his death agreed that no details of a plan were discussed at the case conference and no details of a plan were recorded in the minutes of the case conference. The authors of the inquiry report concluded that failure to formulate a child protection plan left Caleb at risk:

> The follow up to the case conference is a sorry tale of an absence of decision making. There should have been an urgent meeting of the Case Co-ordinator and the other case worker to agree a proper Child Protection Plan and a co-ordinated approach to monitoring Caleb. No decision was taken to arrange one. (O'Brien *et al.*, 2003)

Kennedy McFarlane was discharged from hospital with no clear follow-up plan being put in place. The issues surrounding the care and protection of Kennedy were discussed at a planning meeting but no clear actions were agreed to address them. There was no plan for a formal joint investigation with the police or a referral to the Reporter and no multi-agency care plan was formulated. It was later decided that a case conference should be held and that the case should be referred to the Reporter but the child protection referral form failed to highlight the extent of known concerns to Kennedy's safety and there was no clear plan to investigate her circumstances or protect her while the case conference was being arranged.

LEARNING POINTS

✔ **Professionals need extensive training in and appreciation of child development and attachment theory, as well as training in key knowledge concerning factors such as substance misuse, mental illness and domestic violence. They also need a theoretical model for analysis as well as a structure for collecting key information if they are to undertake comprehensive assessments of children's needs for care and protection.**

✔ **Information about the ways in which parents looked after other children, who may have been taken into care, should be taken into account when assessing parenting skills. The parenting/caring abilities of fathers and significant males needs to be given more weight in assessment.**

✔ **Families do not have to engage unless thresholds of significant harm are reached. Reasons for refusal to engage should be explored and agencies may need to consider more effective, creative ways of engaging some young people and families.**

COMMUNICATION

Findings from England and Wales

▤ Ofsted (2008a) highlighted examples of poor communication between agencies; in contrast, other research has highlighted examples of extensive communication (Brandon *et al.*, 2008; Rose and Barnes, 2008; Owers *et al.*, 1999; Brandon *et al.*, 2002).

▤ Ofsted (2008a) and Owers *et al.* (1999) found examples of weaknesses in communication and information sharing within universal services, particularly health.

▤ Ofsted (2008a) found that in some cases no single agency had a complete picture of the family and a full record of the concern; they also identified problems with communication when families moved.

▤ Brandon *et al.* (2008) and Owers *et al.* (1999) found that professionals were sometimes reluctant to challenge the opinion of other professionals.

▤ Rose and Barnes (2008) and Brandon *et al.* (2002) found that important professionals were sometimes excluded from meetings.

▤ Brandon *et al.* (2002) found examples of failure to share information in relation to domestic violence.

Inter-agency communication

Relevant information about a child may be held by different agencies or by different individuals within the same agency. Effective communication and information sharing across and between agencies is, therefore, crucial in protecting children. Communication has been identified as a major theme in most inquiries and reviews. The inquiry report into the death of Victoria Climbie found that information was shared across agencies but professionals were often reluctant to challenge professionals from other agencies, particularly doctors.

Some examples of good inter-agency communication were identified in the Scottish inquiry and review reports. The authors of the Carla Nicole Bone report commented that inter-agency collaboration was generally good. In Eilean Siar social work agencies, health centres, clinics, schools, nurseries and family centres constantly shared information and communicated concerns about the family in formal meetings, as well as informally, but 'the children were disadvantaged by the apparent absence of debate amongst all the professionals involved and between professionals and members of the children's hearing'.

Examples of inadequate inter-agency communication between health and social work, education and health, social work and the police, and between adult and child services were identified in the Scottish reports (Orkney, Caleb Ness, Kennedy McFarlane, Danielle Reid, Colyn Evans). The inquiry into the death of Caleb Ness identified a number of examples where communication between health and social work was problematic:

- Health professionals did not tell social workers that Caleb's mother was pregnant even though she had a serious heroin addiction.

- Health professionals did not inform social work of Caleb's mother's failure to attend appointments or of her increased prescription.

- The health visitor notified the social worker and GP about Shirley's post-natal depression and refusal of antidepressants but the social worker did not act on this information.

- There was no joint protocol between social work and health that recognised and planned for the special needs of babies with neonatal abstinence syndrome.

- The social worker and health visitor did not work together to monitor Caleb once he went home.

Intra-agency communication

Communication within health was identified as problematic in the Victoria Climbie Inquiry report. Poor intra-agency communication was similarly identified in a number of the Scottish inquiry and review reports. The link between pre-school and school health services was identified as problematic in the Eilean Siar and Danielle Reid review reports. Health visitors' notes are normally passed to the school nurse when a child starts school but health visitors' notes were lost for the family in Eilean Siar because no school nurse was in post at the time. Communication between different parts of the health service was also identified as an issue in the Caleb Ness and Kennedy McFarlane inquiry reports. Even though Caleb Ness was on the Child Protection Register the health visitor was not given advance warning of his discharge from hospital. Problems in the interface between adult health services and child services, particularly in the fields of brain injury and substance misuse, were also highlighted as an issue in the report of the inquiry into Caleb's death.

Information sharing between different parts of the social work service was identified as problematic in some inquiry and review reports (Caleb Ness, Danielle Reid). The review into the death of Danielle Reid found that the computerised system did not allow speedy and accurate sharing of information across the social work department. Social workers did not have adequate training to ensure information in relation to potential risk to children was cross-checked through the various departments so information, particularly from criminal justice, was not always passed to children and families. New electronic information-sharing systems should help solve these kinds of technical problems provided staff receive relevant training in how to operate them effectively.

Transferring information between areas

Information transfer and communication can be particularly problematic when families move. There may be particular issues around information transfer when families move to the UK from abroad. The inquiry into the death of Victoria Climbie found that social services did not attempt to verify any aspect of Victoria and her great-aunt's life before her arrival in England. No checks were made on the other children her great-aunt said she had in France. It was only after Victoria's death that information came to light that Victoria had been known to social services and her school had registered a Child at Risk Emergency Notification with the French education authorities because of her repeated absence from school.

None of the children in the Scottish inquiry and review reports had moved to Scotland from abroad but some had moved from England and problems around the transfer of information were identified even where families had moved between local authority or health board areas in Scotland (Dunblane, Colyn Evans, Caleb Ness, Eilean Siar, Carla Nicole Bone). Social services staff in England provided social work staff in Eilean Siar with extensive information about the family. Copies of child protection case conference minutes were transferred but case files containing important information that would have affected the risk assessment which was undertaken on the father remained in England. Health files were eventually transferred but not in time for the first case conference.

Particular problems around information transfer were identified in the Danielle Reid review report. Danielle's mother, Tracy, had been referred to social work as an adolescent and was later referred to the learning disability team but social work services had no records of these contacts. There were also problems in the transfer of health information relating to Danielle. Danielle's family moved many times and health notes did not always follow the family timeously. On some occasions notes did not follow them at all:

notes were never moved to the Dundee area and there was a delay in acquiring child health notes on arrival in Inverness. Information transfer was also an issue in education. Danielle Reid's mother informed Danielle's school that Danielle was moving to England but there were no systems checks in place in the education system at that time to ensure a child had been enrolled in a new school. The report of the review into Danielle's death expressed the need for a formal tracking system, on a UK basis, within the education system. It also recommended immediate transfer of information between education and health, and vice versa, if it became known that a child had moved from the area.

Information from the public

It's Everyone's Job to Make Sure I'm Alright (Scottish Executive, 2002), the report of the National Audit and Review of Child Protection in Scotland, emphasised the important role the community has to play in protecting children. Agencies rely on members of the public to share information with them, particularly where they have no contact with children themselves. Information from the public appeared to play only a very minimal role in any of the key cases in Scotland. At the trials into the deaths of Carla Nicole Bone and Danielle Reid neighbours provided information which would have been very significant to agencies in terms of assessing the level of risk to these children but neighbours had been reluctant to report their concerns at the time. If child protection really is 'everyone's job' then the community must share some of the responsibility for the death of these children if they were aware of abuse and neglect but failed to report it.

Confidentiality

The issue of what information professionals are able to share due to confidentiality was raised in the Victoria Climbie Inquiry report:

> Throughout this inquiry it was said repeatedly that when there is professional concern about the welfare of a child, the free exchange of information is inhibited by the Data Protection Act 1998, the Human Rights Act 1998, and common law rules on confidentiality. The evidence put to the inquiry was that unless a child is deemed to be in need of protection, information cannot be shared between agencies without staff running the risk that their actions are unlawful … There must be a balance struck between the protection of a child and the right to privacy. (Laming, 2003)

Whether or not a case is defined as a child protection case may affect the extent to which information is shared between professionals. Some of the professionals who were interviewed in the Scottish inquiries and reviews reported that information-sharing protocols were unclear when child protection issues had not been raised. Some of the professionals who were interviewed in the Caleb Ness Inquiry reported that they did not seek information from adult services because they did not think it would be forthcoming: Alexander Ness's criminal justice worker failed to seek information from his doctor; and Shirley Malcolm's addiction worker knew Shirley Malcolm was under stress but did not see it as his duty to pass that information to Caleb's case co-ordinator. Professionals who were interviewed for the Danielle Reid review reported that they were reluctant to share information in relation to adults, particularly information relating to adult mental health, drug and alcohol addiction or learning difficulties, unless a child protection investigation was underway. They expressed confusion about what information could be shared at meetings which were not child protection meetings:

> It is clear from interviews with staff that information sharing with other agencies is an obstacle to appropriate child protection especially when children have not entered formal 'child protection' procedures. Formalised child protection procedures are perceived by health staff to be the threshold for sharing confidential information. (Herbison, 2005)

The author of the review report concluded that 'Unless agencies are confident that they can share information relevant to children's exposure to risk of harm without breach of legislation or Human Rights, then children are exposed to unnecessary risk'.

Electronic information-sharing systems

UK governments have responded to the findings of inquiries and reviews by seeking to address problems around communication through the introduction of electronic information-sharing systems that can be accessed by all agencies. While information-sharing databases may assist in the collection of information, they are unlikely to solve the significant problems around communication that have been highlighted in inquiries and reviews. Munro (2005) points out that criticisms in relation to professional failure to share information are actually relatively rare in inquiry reports after 1979. In later reports criticisms centre instead on failure to assess shared information accurately and information-sharing databases are unlikely to be of much assistance in this task.

CASE

Staff from all agencies reported that issues of confidentiality, client access to records and data protection were inhibitors for recording and sharing information in relation to Carla Nicole Bone. When Carla's mother's partner joined the family the social work department made some checks in their own records about him but did not feel they had any legitimate reason to seek detailed information about him from other agencies.

> When a family comes to seek help on a voluntary basis staff do not feel it is appropriate to make extensive checks unless they have the permission of the adults or there is a major concern about the welfare of the child. It is of note that in Carla's case the appropriate threshold to make extensive checks was not reached. Such major concerns being present would override the parents' rights to refuse the collection of such information and their right to privacy. (North East of Scotland Child Protection Committee, 2003)

The authors of the review report point out that the tracking of sex offenders has been given high priority but tracking adults that pose other dangers to children has not been covered by guidance or legislation because issues of confidentiality and the rights of adults to privacy make it difficult to reach agreement about this dangerous group:

> Retaining more information on adults who may present a danger to children will also mean the rights of some adults being sacrificed to better protect children. If society wants to protect children more effectively, however, adults need to give up some of their rights to privacy to enable such checks to be made. (North East of Scotland Child Protection Commmittee, 2003)

Practice implications

Professionals need clear guidelines in relation to the sharing of information when child protection thresholds have not been met.

LEARNING POINTS

✔ **Practitioners should be encouraged to exercise professional discretion and challenge decisions within and between agencies.**

✔ **Campaigns to encourage communities to share information should be ongoing.**

RECORD KEEPING AND ACCOUNTABILITY

Findings from England and Wales

🗐 A number of researchers have identified examples of inadequate record keeping in universal services (Ofsted, 2008a; Owers *et al.*, 1999; Brandon *et al.*, 2002; Brandon *et al.*, 2008) and examples of illegible, unsigned, lost or missing records (Ofsted, 2008a; Owers *et al.*, 1999; Brandon *et al.*, 2002; Brandon *et al.*, 2008):

🗐 Ofsted (2008a) and Owers *et al.* (1999) found examples of poor knowledge and application of policies and procedures.

🗐 Owers *et al.* (1999) identified problems with the transfer of records when families move.

🗐 Owers *et al.* (1999) found that agencies did not always recognise they had responsibility for child protection.

Records

The inquiry report into the death of Victoria Climbie identified significant problems in relation to record keeping. During Victoria's brief involvement with Brent social services, partly as a result of the children's social work department running both manual systems and a separate client-based computer system, Victoria acquired five different identifier numbers. There was also a lack of adequate record keeping by hospital staff with information being kept in a variety of different places. Photographs were taken which demonstrated a clear record of the marks on Victoria's body but no-one saw them until after Victoria's death because there was no adequate system for distributing photographs.

The authors of the systematic review into historical abuse in Scotland highlighted the importance of records for contributing to informed decision making about keeping children safe and responding to claims of abuse. Locating information for the purposes of undertaking the systematic review itself proved both challenging and time consuming. 'This review experienced difficulty in addressing its remit due to the poor state of records associated with children's residential services. Future inquiries will also be affected unless proper records management practices are universally adopted' (Bell, 2007, p. 214).

Problems around record keeping in social work, the police, health and SCRA were identified in the Scottish inquiry and review reports (Caleb Ness, Kennedy McFarlane, Orkney, Colyn Evans, Danielle Reid). There were frequent references to information being mislaid, destroyed or lost. Records which were kept were often inadequate and there were numerous references to mistakes in the minutes of meetings.

The absence of records or notes of meetings held and decisions taken was identified as a major deficiency in the Orkney case. The social work department in Orkney was small and staff tended to discuss things informally meaning very few written records were kept:

- There was no written record of the interviews with the three children who made the allegations.
- There was no written record of the decision to seek Place of Safety Orders.
- There were no individual case files for the nine children.
- Notes were taken in some of the interviews with the nine children but these varied in content and quality.
- The interviewers failed to arrange to have full facilities available for recording and management failed to check that recording facilities were being used.

As in the systemic review of historical abuse in Scotland, the absence of records in Orkney hampered the progress of the inquiry team: 'The Inquiry was left to piece together the history from the informal records which had been kept by some of those most closely involved and from their recollections.'

The recent Inquiry into abuse at Kerelaw Residential School and Secure Unit also pointed to problems with the quality of records. There were many examples of different spellings of children's names and different dates of birth: 'In some case files the recording was so poor it was not possible to establish the frequency of contact between the worker and the child. Nor was it always clear what work was being carried out' (Frizzell, 2009, p. 90).

Numerous problems in relation to record keeping were identified in the Caleb Ness Inquiry report:

- The minute taker at the case conference had never taken minutes before and had no training in how to carry out that role.
- The date on the minutes was wrong.
- Caleb's name was recorded as 'Kalib'.
- There is confusion in the minutes over who attended and who was absent.
- The minute implies throughout that Caleb should go home as though the decision had been made somewhere else at another time.
- The minutes were not checked by the chair.
- The minutes were not typed up until after Caleb had died so were not distributed to the relevant professionals who attended.
- Some of the inquiry witnesses claimed a key decision that Alexander Ness

would not be left alone in charge of the baby was made but this was not recorded in the minutes.

- The summary sheet the health visitor was sent from the hospital reporting the birth of Caleb Ness stated that the baby was a girl.

- GPs and health visitors were linked by a computer software system where information could be shared but the software did not allow for a page relating to child protection so the health visitor's cause for concern records could not be accessed through it and GPs had no access to health visitors' computerised records.

ACCOUNTABILITY

A number of the Scottish inquiry and review reports identified problems in relation to accountability in health (Kennedy McFarlane, Eilean Siar, Caleb Ness, Danielle Reid). Lines of accountability in health were sometimes unclear. The Eilean Siar review report concluded that the Health Board did not have the systems in place to support health professionals in protecting children.

Basic police procedures were not followed in relation to Danielle Reid. The police became involved when a family member rang them to say no one had seen Danielle for three months: 'Despite the seriousness of the content of the phone call made by family member 6 that the child had died, there was complete breakdown of standardised practice at every level, particularly in relation to a missing vulnerable child.' Danielle had already been killed by this time and the review report states that nothing done at this point could have saved her life but the author of the report expressed concern that basic procedures were not followed.

RESPONSIBILITY

It's Everyone's Job to Make Sure I'm Alright (Scottish Executive, 2002), the report of the National Audit and Review of Child Protection in Scotland, emphasised that all agencies have a responsibility for child protection but evidence from some of the inquiries and reviews that have reported since then suggests that agencies may not have been aware of this responsibility. For example, the criminal justice social worker who worked with Alexander Ness thought his role was about the rehabilitation of Alexander. Everything to do with Caleb he dismissed as the responsibility of the children and families team. The authors of the Caleb Ness Inquiry report commented that:

some professionals failed to acknowledge their own responsibilities for identifying and responding to child protection concerns ... there was a complete failure by Criminal Justice workers and management to recognise that they did have some responsibility for child protection. Similarly, we saw an incomplete understanding of their role in child protection in the actions of addiction professionals and brain injury specialists, who are accustomed to working with adult patients. (O'Brien *et al.*, 2003)

When Colyn Evans's supervision requirement was terminated, his pathway plan was around management of finances, employment and accommodation but no-one took responsibility for managing risk. The throughcare team did not believe they had a role in relation to risk management. The CSS team had a remit to provide intervention for his sexually inappropriate behaviour but also failed to view themselves as having a responsibility for risk management.

LEARNING POINT

✔ **Recording should be about more than describing events. It should also document decision making and planning processes.**

STAFFING ISSUES

Findings from England and Wales

- A number of research reports have highlighted examples of staff in universal and adult services failing to identify and report signs of abuse (Ofsted, 2008a; Sinclair and Bullock, 2002; Owers *et al.*, 1999).
- A number of research reports have identified lack of management oversight/supervision (Ofsted, 2008a; Brandon *et al.*, 2008; Rose and Barnes, 2008; Sinclair and Bullock, 2002; Owers *et al.*, 1999; Brandon *et al.*, 2002).
- Brandon *et al.* 2002 and 2008 identified lack of resources, e.g. social workers carrying high numbers of cases as an issue; in contrast, Ofsted (2008a), Sinclair and Bullock (2002) and Owers *et al.* (1999) found that resources played less of a part than might have been expected.

Supervision

Inadequate supervision was identified as an issue in the Victoria Climbie Inquiry report. The system of supervision in the police was inadequate and social services staff did not receive satisfactory levels of supervision. Inadequate supervision of staff was identified as an issue in a high proportion of the Scottish inquiry and review reports (Eilean Siar, Carla Nicole Bone,

Caleb Ness, Kennedy McFarlane, Richard Clark, Orkney, Kerelaw). The team manager in the Kennedy McFarlane case never mentioned the case to her line manager in their monthly supervision sessions. The Caleb Ness Inquiry report also noted lack of supervision in social work. Caleb was mentioned in supervision sessions but the authors of the inquiry report concluded that discussions held in supervision sessions were routine and superficial and the notes which were taken of the sessions were 'scanty and inexact'.

Supervision is important because it is useful for a new person to take a fresh look at the evidence and another person's perspective can improve the quality of assessment. Inquiries have shown how persistently professionals can hold onto their beliefs despite a growing mountain of evidence to the contrary and supervision helps professionals consider alternative points of view (Munro, 1999; Reder and Duncan, 1999). Owers *et al.* (1999) point out, however, that supervision should be about more than management and accountability, it should also be about supporting staff.

> Although supervision has a pivotal role in supporting workers in their day to day activities, when staff struggle to cope with the emotional effects of child protection work, it may become necessary in some instances to supplement such support mechanisms. (p. 48)

Working with vulnerable families has a high emotional impact on practitioners, especially when families are reluctant to engage and difficult to work with (Morrison, 1990) and supervision should enable exploration of the emotional effects of the work. Frizzell (2009) points to the need for staff in residential care to be supported emotionally in coping with challenging and vulnerable young people in order to avoid burn out and the risk of a 'hardening' of approach. The 21st Century Social Work Review in Scotland Changing Lives (Scottish Executive, 2006) set out a new approach to supervision. It suggested that 'consultation' which includes performance management, staff development and staff support was a better approach than supervision alone. However, as Frizzell (2009) points out, 'the effectiveness of "consultation", like "supervision", will be dependent on the commitment of managers at all levels to engage with appropriate frequency and professionalism' (p. 63).

Skills, experience and knowledge of child protection

The inquiry report into the death of Victoria Climbie found that many of the officers employed in child protection teams in the police had not received CID training or child protection training. The PC who was given Victoria's case after she was admitted to hospital with suspected non-accidental injuries did not have sufficient training or experience to deal with the case. She failed to undertake a proper investigation, did not interview Victoria, left hospital staff to interview the childminder and allowed a social worker to speak to Victoria's great-aunt alone. Inexperience was also an issue in social services. Many of the staff in social services were inexperienced temporary agency staff from overseas who had not had sufficient training.

The earlier inquiry and review reports in Scotland all concluded that social workers had insufficient skills or expertise (Richard Clark, Orkney, Edinburgh). The Richard Clark report was published more than 30 years ago when social workers tended to be generic and we might have expected them to have less child protection experience than social workers in children and families teams today. However, some of the more recent inquiry and review reports have also highlighted lack of expertise and experience among social workers:

- The Kennedy McFarlane Inquiry report concluded that social workers needed more training in risk assessment, decision making and legal processes.

- Questions were raised about the level of skill and expertise of staff working with young sexual abusers in the Colyn Evans review report.

- The Eilean Siar review report revealed that insufficient numbers of social work staff were trained in investigative interviewing.

- Both the Caleb Ness and Eilean Siar reports concluded that social work staff had insufficient experience to chair important decision-making meetings.

Since universal services such as education and health and adult services may be the first to have contact with vulnerable children and their families, staff in these services require skills and training in child protection in order to identify and help prevent abuse and neglect. Back in 1991 the Edinburgh Inquiry pointed out that criminal justice and community care staff might be the recipients of reports of historic abuse and needed to know what to do if they found themselves in this situation: 'Social workers working specifically with children and families are not the only ones who need to know about children. Criminal justice social workers have a crucial role to play; as have those working in community care.'

Evidence from more recent review reports suggests that social workers in criminal justice and community care continue to lack knowledge of child protection. The inquiry report into the death of Caleb Ness revealed that the criminal justice workers who worked with Caleb's family had no training in child protection. They were expected to know the basics from social work training but had received no further post-qualifying training.

Also back in 1991 the Orkney Inquiry report recommended that teachers should be trained in the recognition of child sexual abuse. More than a decade later, however, inadequate training in child protection for education staff was highlighted in both the Eilean Siar and Danielle Reid review reports.

> Education staff may be the first to notice that there is cause for concern about a child. In the case of Danielle Reid they were the only service in regular contact ... Education staff require training in order to fulfil a vital role in the task of protecting children. (Herbison, 2005)

The more recent review reports also included references to lack of knowledge of child protection by health staff. The Caleb Ness report concluded that the primary care trust failed to discharge its duty to inform and train its own staff about child protection. It was doing a good job in training and supervising health visitors but the psychiatrists, psychologist, GPs and outreach nurse involved with Caleb were not trained in child protection.

Resources

Resources were identified as a significant issue in the Victoria Climbie Inquiry report. At the time Victoria's case was being handled by Brent Council, all the duty social workers had received their training abroad and were on temporary contracts; several workers in the child protection team had also been recruited on a temporary basis. The inquiry into Victoria's death was told that 'There were occasions where a person will get off a plane in the morning, arrive in the office just after lunch, be interviewed and start work either in the duty team or the child protection team. It was happening very, very often.'

One of the social workers who was allocated Victoria's case in Haringey was responsible for 19 cases, half of which were child protection (seven more cases than the maximum recommended in procedural guidance). This social worker had never completed a Section 47 inquiry, never dealt with a child in hospital and never taken a case through to case conference. No assessment was made as to whether she had the requisite capabilities to handle the case and no consideration was taken of whether her workload would allow her to devote enough time to Victoria's case.

While staff shortages have probably never reached the same level of crisis in Scotland as they did in some of the London boroughs that were involved in the Victoria Climbie case, they were identified as problematic in some inquiry and review reports (Danielle Reid, Orkney, Colyn Evans, Carla Nicole Bone, Kerelaw). The authors of the Danielle Reid report went so far as to conclude that staffing shortages in social work services were at an unsafe level. Some staff had not undertaken child protection training and the frequency of supervision had been reduced because of staff shortages. Home visits were prioritised on a workload rather than a needs basis and case notes were being handwritten and could not then be transferred onto the computer system. In the police levels of staffing during public holidays and at weekends were identified as a contributory factor in the failure to respond appropriately and timeously.

An issue which has been highlighted in several of the Scottish inquiry and review reports is the extent to which smaller, more rural areas have the range of resources and expertise to provide a full range of services to vulnerable families and children needing protection (Carla Nicole Bone, Eilean Siar, Orkney, Kennedy McFarlane). In Eilean Siar the full extent of the services offered to the family in England could not be matched by the much more limited resources of a remote part of Scotland and the authors of the review report questioned whether the local authority had the range of expertise to address complex child abuse issues. In Orkney the children had to be taken to the mainland because of an absence of resources in Orkney:

> the Department which was required to face the problem was a very small one and lacked the expertise to recognise or deal with the full complexity of the situation which faced it. The level of expertise needed in cases of such complexity is high and unlikely to be found in more than a relatively few members of staff even in large authorities ... It might be questioned whether the Social Work Department fully realised the enormity of the task which they undertook ... It was an enterprise which ... would have stretched local resources in Strathclyde. It was an enterprise of a stressful character demanding considerable resource, far beyond what the tiny Department in Orkney could manage. (Clyde, 1992)

The author of the Kennedy McFarlane report questioned whether what happened to Kennedy would have happened elsewhere. There are issues around equity if it cannot be ensured that children receive the same levels of protection across Scotland. The fact that children have died or been seriously abused in cities as well as smaller, more rural areas in Scotland suggests children are unlikely to be at higher risk in rural areas. It is, however, interesting that none of the key public inquiries or reviews in Scotland have concerned children living in Glasgow, when it is the largest city in Scotland and comprises a fifth of the total population. Glasgow City Council was responsible for the stewardship of Kerelaw Residential School and Secure Unit but Kerelaw was actually situated in North Ayrshire. Unlike some of the smaller local authorities, however, Glasgow undertook Significant Case Reviews prior to the issue of national guidance in 2007 so it may be that cases of child death and serious abuse in Glasgow were reviewed via local, internal case review processes rather than through public inquiries or reviews.

LEARNING POINTS

✔ **Supervision should be available to staff in all agencies.**

✔ **Supervision should include supporting practitioners to cope with the emotional demands of work with children and families as well as checking and accountability.**

✔ **Staff in universal and adult services play a key role in keeping children safe. It is vitally important that they have the necessary skills and knowledge to identify and respond to signs of abuse.**

WORKING WITH PARENTS

Findings from England and Wales

▤ Ofsted (2008a) found that professionals sometimes took the word of parents at face value and did not question their version of events.

▤ A number of research reports have found that professionals are often over-optimistic about parenting capacity, accept standards of care that would not be acceptable in other families and became 'desensitised' to poor conditions within the home (Rose and Barnes, 2008; Ofsted, 2008a; Brandon *et al.*, 2008; Brandon *et al.*, 2002).

▤ Brandon *et al.* (2008) found that apparent or disguised cooperation from parents prevented or delayed understanding of the severity of harm to the child.

▤ Ofsted (2008a) and Brandon *et al.* (2008) found that professionals were sometimes frightened to visit homes due to hostility from adults.

Balancing parents' and children's rights

Professionals are increasingly being encouraged to work with whole families, with children and with adults, but there can be tensions in balancing the rights of parents and children.

There were numerous examples in the Scottish inquiry and review reports of professionals focusing on parents' and carers' needs rather than those of children, professionals believing at face value adults' explanations for injuries and absences from school, and adults' rights generally taking precedence over those of children. The social worker in the Richard Clark case was criticised for giving more weight to Richard's carers' rights than to Richard's right to protection. She did not consider the needs of Richard and his brother separately from those of the adults. The family friends with whom Richard and his brother were placed were known to have neglected their own children. A voluntary sector worker who was involved with the family expressed concern that Richard and his brother would be an unfair burden on a couple struggling to care for their own children but the social worker responded that it would be unfair to condemn the couple because of their past history. The inquiry report into the abuse suffered by Richard Clark is interesting in that it considered Richard's parents' responsibilities in relation to what happened as well as those of professionals. None of the subsequent inquiries and reviews have considered the responsibilities of family members. The Richard Clark Inquiry concluded that Richard's father had considerable cause for anxiety about Richard's safety and should, like the social worker, have made greater efforts to have him removed from the carers' home.

Thirty years after the Richard Clark Inquiry, the Eilean Siar report made similar comments in relation to professionals needing to balance the weight given to the rights of parents against the needs and rights of children. Professionals in Eilean Siar were more willing to believe the accounts of adult family members about what was happening at home than those of the children. The professional response to the family was to provide services to support the parents to bring up the children themselves. The authors of the review report point out that this is in keeping with the principles of the Children (Scotland) Act 1995, which states that so far as is consistent with safeguarding and promoting the child's welfare the local authority must promote the upbringing of children by their families. They comment that the principles of the Children (Scotland) Act 1995 and the aftermath of the Orkney Inquiry may have contributed to the prolonged attempts to engage with the family rather than try to remove the three children. They conclude, however, that in families where serious abuse continues to occur this approach, while consistent with the principles of the Children (Scotland) Act 1995, is not consistent with safeguarding children's welfare.

The Orkney Inquiry did not conclude that parents' rights took precedence. Indeed one of the main reasons for undertaking the Orkney Inquiry was professionals' failure to uphold parents' rights. In stark contrast to the findings of the other inquiries and reviews that were undertaken in Scotland the authors of the Orkney report concluded that the social work department prioritised the children and did not support the parents:

- Parents were not invited to the case conference, were unable to contribute their views in writing and were not informed of the outcome of the conference.

- Contrary to what was recognised as good practice no visits were made to the parents.

- Parents were refused access to their children, did not know where they were and were not told whether they were placed with their siblings.

- Parents were not given copies of the Place of Safety Orders or given any other documents explaining the procedure and setting out their rights.

- Parental consent, or otherwise, to medically examine the children was not noted in writing and the results of the medical examination were not conveyed to the parents.

- Mail that the parents sent to their children was vetted and not always forwarded to them.

- There was no clear procedure for parents to pursue complaints to the local authority.

CASE

The authors of the Carla Nicole Bone report comment that because Carla's mother was seen as loving this clouded professionals' views of the quality of the physical and emotional care she was providing. Intervention was focused on the vulnerabilities of the parent rather than the child. The authors of the report found little evidence of anyone challenging Carla's mother about the unacceptable standards of Carla's care and she was not given a clear message about when her care was falling short of acceptable standards.

Some of the professionals expressed concerns about challenging Carla's mother in case she disappeared, since a family can withdraw at any time if services are being provided voluntarily. The authors question whether parents should be given a choice about whether or not they should or should not attend programmes if their level of care is assessed as poor or inadequate: 'It may be that there were no grounds for child protection systems to be started but if a child's care does not improve then parents need to know that statutory powers may be introduced.'

Lack of parental cooperation or unwillingness to accept help raises problems for interventions below the threshold for child protection concerns where the state has no mandate to intervene compulsorily and families must agree to agency involvement.

Practice implication

If a family fails to attend appointments or refuses to take up a service the child requires this should be taken into account in assessment and professionals should consider raising the status of the case to a higher, child protection threshold.

Believing what parents say

There is a section in the Victoria Climbie Inquiry report headed 'Working with deceitful people' in which Lord Laming talks about the extent to which professionals accepted at face value what Victoria's great-aunt told them. Her claim that she was Victoria's mother was never challenged and no proof ever sought but if anyone had asked to see Victoria's passport they would have seen that the child in the photograph looked nothing like her. Rustin (2005) comments that it is remarkable how successful Victoria's great-aunt was in her endeavour to persuade doctors, social workers, police and others to see things as she saw them: 'the impact of *her* confusion and distortion of the truth seems to have invaded the minds of those who came into contact with her ... Instead of being able to observe and thus question Kouao's belief system, workers began to mirror it' (p. 12).

There are numerous examples of professionals too readily believing what parents told them in the Scottish inquiry and review reports. The school believed Danielle Reid's mother's excuses for her non-attendance. Because she was registered blind Tracy Reid was able to provide a verbal report to the school to account for absences rather than written statements. After Danielle's death it became apparent that her mother deliberately deceived education staff in relation to her absences from school.

Social workers were also criticised in the inquiry report into the death of Caleb Ness for believing at face value everything they were told by Caleb Ness's mother:

> There was an unspoken assumption that the parents had the right to care for their baby. This dominated events to the extent that Caleb's right to a safe and secure upbringing was never the focus of decision making ... Because of the favourable impression that Shirley made on him, he dismissed her truly appalling history of past parenting.
> (O'Brien *et al.*, 2003)

Over-optimism regarding parents' capacity to change

Professionals were over-optimistic about adults' capacity to change in several of the Scottish inquiry and review reports. The authors of the Caleb Ness Inquiry report comment that the case conference held for Caleb Ness failed to ask the question 'what evidence was there for a change in Shirley's lifestyle or behaviour which suggested she would be a safe parent'.

The main issue which should have been discussed at the case conference should have been whether to send Caleb home at all but this was never examined properly because of an over-optimistic view about Shirley's drug use.

Inquiries and reviews have demonstrated the lengths which people will go to in their attempts to deceive practitioners. Professionals believed that Colyn Evans's behaviour had improved but evidence presented in the review suggests he deceived them because he was aware that he would be allowed to go home if he was able to demonstrate progress:

> In this way he took the 'pole' position in his relationship with his supervising social worker and the record indicates his ability to 'play the game' to achieve the outcome he wished. Given the speed with which his home situation broke down and his refusal to participate in any intervention programme, it seems reasonable to suppose that the view taken by the social workers involved was overly optimistic. (SWIA/HMIC, 2005)

Over-optimism regarding parents' capacity to change was also a significant feature of the Eilean Siar case:

> Throughout the children's lives professionals were often over-optimistic about the capacity of members of family A to overcome their disadvantaged and abusive childhoods, manage their own mental and physical health problems, cope with poverty and poor housing and nurture and protect their children. (SWIA, 2005)

The authors of the review report concluded that:

> In families where serious abuse occurs and the adults are not willing and able to change sufficiently within timescales important to the child, decisions need to be made to separate them from their children. The extent of the resources being provided and the willingness of parents to 'cooperate' with workers do not in themselves indicate improved parenting. (SWIA, 2005)

LEARNING POINTS

✔ **Practitioners need significant levels of support to work with hostile and aggressive parents.**

✔ **Abusive parents may also be, or appear to be, loving parents.**

✔ **When there is insufficient evidence of demonstrable change in a child's circumstances and well-being, agencies may need to act to safeguard the child.**

FOCUS ON THE CHILD

Findings from England and Wales

▧ Rose and Barnes (2008) and Brandon *et al.* (2008) found examples of professionals focusing on adults' needs rather than children's.

▧ Ofsted (2008a) found that professionals did not always consider the situation from the child's perspective. They did not record how children were, what they said or how they looked, or document changes in their behaviour or appearance.

▧ Ofsted (2008a), Rose and Barnes (2008) and Brandon *et al.* (2002) found that professionals did not always see or speak to the child and listen to, or take account of, his or her views.

Talking and listening to children

Back in the 1980s the Jasmine Beckford Inquiry (Butler and Drakeford, 2003) in England was critical of social workers for regarding the parents of children in care as the clients rather than the children. Twenty years later the inquiry into the death of Victoria Climbie made similar criticisms of social workers who barely spoke to Victoria and focused all their attention on her great-aunt. The police were also criticised for failing to interview Victoria despite criminal allegations being made. The only reason Victoria's great-aunt was referred to Ealing Social Services was because of Victoria's needs, yet professionals largely ignored her needs and Victoria was never viewed as the client. Rustin (2005) points out, however, that talking to children may be a difficult task for professionals: 'A capacity for communicating with children is expected of social workers and of police officers involved in child protection, but this is by no means an easy task' (p. 15).

It may be difficult for adults to find a way of communicating with a child to whom they are a virtual stranger. Rustin comments that working out who can be trusted would be a very difficult task for a child in Victoria's situation 'and the "authorities" are not in the least likely to appear trustworthy' (p. 16). She concludes that 'Without the involvement of teachers or others in the community who know a child over time, the professional task of child protection is up against exceptional odds' (p. 16).

In Scotland the inquiry into the abuse suffered by Richard Clark criticised social workers for not attempting to get Richard and his brother to talk about their feelings. The Fife Enquiry also found that children were not asked their views on how they were or what their hopes were for their future care.

The Edinburgh Inquiry report noted that adults' rights were given more weight than children's: 'employment law and the policy focus on supporting adults with alcohol difficulties moved the focus inappropriately from the needs of children to the needs and rights of the adult employees'.

It emerged during the course of the Edinburgh Inquiry that a number of children had made reports to members of staff but they had not been taken seriously and no action had been taken. Some former residents told the inquiry that they had not been believed. They described how children would climb a tree near the staff window shouting 'Brian's a perv', presumably in an attempt to alert staff to what was happening to them, but were simply told to come down and behave themselves. The inquiry heard that one ex-resident had written a poem which she showed to a member of staff in an attempt to alert them to what was happening to her, but staff again failed to identify this as a cry for help. Children often ran away from Clerwood but staff did not attempt to find out why. The authors of the report concluded that:

> We make no criticism of staff at that time for not having identified the name calling as a potential cry for help. However, the lesson to be learned is that any child, and particularly a young child, may experience difficulty in articulating complaints against staff in relation to inappropriate behaviour by them. (Marshall *et al.*, 1999)

The recent systemic review of historical abuse in Scotland concluded that up until the 1980s the law did not provide adequately for talking and listening to children and taking their views into account. There was also little awareness at the time that adults could engage in sexually abusive behaviour, and this would have made it difficult for children to talk about sexual abuse and difficult for adults to identify the signs of abuse. While staff involved in the Edinburgh Inquiry and Fife Enquiry would have had limited awareness of sexual abuse at the time and it would not have been routine practice to talk to and listen to children, there is evidence from the far more recent Eilean Siar review report to suggest that children are still not listened to routinely. At various points all three of the girls in the family in Eilean Siar appeared to be trying to tell adults outside the family that they were being abused but they were not listened to. Children's hearings regularly decided not to appoint a safeguarder but the authors of the review report concluded that a safeguarder might have been useful in enabling the girls to communicate with professionals.

The recent inquiry into abuse at Kerelaw Residential School and Secure Unit which investigated historical abuse, as well as more recent abuse this century, concluded that in a residential setting it is crucial that workers 'embrace a child-centred approach, in which children are listened to, their needs respected and their vulnerabilities understood' (Frizzell, 2009, p. 51). At Kerelaw some staff were child-centred and some young people had a positive experience but 'The Inquiry did not gain a sense that the rights, needs and welfare of children were central to the operation of Kerelaw or the actions of all staff who worked there' (Frizzell, 2009, p. 7).

An effective complaints system is of fundamental importance in the protection of children in residential care. There was a complaints system in existence at Kerelaw but the Inquiry found that young people were discouraged from complaining by being told that they would not be believed because of their pasts. Responses to complaints were brief and young people received inadequate feedback. As in the Edinburgh Inquiry young people frequently absconded from Kerelaw but absconding rates were not monitored and no-one considered the possibility that young people may have been absconding because of abuse.

CASE

Children in Orkney were listened to and believed but their rights were infringed in other ways:

Professionals focused on preserving evidence rather than the welfare of the children.

The social work department viewed the nine children as a single case and failed to see each child as an individual.

The children were separated from their siblings, not allowed to take personal possessions and refused access to their parents.

The professionals who interviewed the children did not explain what the purpose of the interviews was, why they were being recorded, or what information would be passed on to others and used in evidence.

The authors of the Orkney report concluded that the law at that time was partly to blame for professionals' failure to uphold children's rights:

The removal of a child from the immediate control or care of the parents constitutes a significant invasion of the rights of the parent and of the child. While power to remove a child requires to be available the limits of its exercise and the definition of its purpose must be certain, must be clearly known and must be appropriate to the seriousness of the course of action. Section 37(2) of the 1968 Act failed to meet these requirements. The vagueness of Section 37(2) which relates to any child 'who is likely to be caused unnecessary suffering or serious impairment of health because there is, or is believed to be, in respect of the child a lack of parental care' leaves open the opportunity to remove a child on the basis of suspicion and uncertainty. It could also be seen to run counter to Article 8 of the European Convention on children's rights under which everyone has the right to respect for their private and family life, home and correspondence, and Article 16 of the UNCRC under which no child shall be subjected to arbitrary or unlawful interference with his or her privacy, family, home or correspondence. Where the case is one only of suspicion and uncertainty removal to a place of safety should not be justifiable. Removal should only be justifiable where there is a real, urgent and immediate risk that the child will otherwise suffer significant harm. (Clyde, 1992)

LEARNING POINTS

✔ **Professionals in all agencies require training in basic skills in communicating with children.**

✔ **Professionals require training in communicating about sensitive matters.**

✔ **Practitioners should ensure that they see and speak to children.**

✔ **Practitioners should be alert to the fact that children may try to report abuse in very subtle ways.**

✔ **Working in partnership with parents is important but children's needs must not be lost or overshadowed.**

✔ **A family support perspective should not obscure the need to ensure children are properly protected.**

CONCLUSION

This chapter looked at agency factors, or factors related to the practice of professionals, which have been identified in inquiries or reviews into child deaths or serious abuse in Scotland and in other parts of the UK. The main findings are:

❑ it is what is done with information, rather than its simple accumulation, that leads to more analytic assessments and safer practice;

❑ assessment of risk and need is an ongoing process;

❑ risk of harm needs to be managed as well as assessed;

❑ assessment of risk should form part of a wider assessment of the whole child including a child's need for care and protection;

❑ assessment of the parenting skills of fathers and significant males is important;

❑ historical information should always be sought and taken into account;

❑ children in need may also be in need of protection;

❑ information-sharing protocols are not always clear about what information can be shared when child protection thresholds have not been met;

❑ information-sharing databases are unlikely to solve the problems around communication that have been highlighted in inquiries and reviews;

❑ decision making and planning processes should be documented;

❑ supervision helps professionals to reflect and consider alternative points of view;

❑ staff need support to cope with the emotional effects of child protection work;

❑ universal and adult services may be the first services to have contact with children and families, and staff in these services need to be able to identify child abuse and neglect;

❑ smaller, more rural areas may not have the range of resources and expertise to provide a full range of services to vulnerable children and families;

❑ professionals need support to work with hostile, manipulative parents and need to feel confident to challenge parents when standards of care are unacceptable;

❑ professionals from all agencies require training in communicating with children;

❑ working in partnership with parents is important but the needs of the child should be the main focus of intervention.

Chapter 6 considers what impact inquiries and reviews have had on child protection policy and practice in Scotland and other parts of the UK.

The impact of inquiries and reviews on child protection policy and practice

Introduction

The impact of inquiries and reviews on child protection policy nationally has been significant. Indeed, they have been one of the main drivers for policy and practice change in Scotland, as well as the rest of the UK. Some of the policy and practice changes that have come about as a result of implementing the recommendations of inquiry and review reports have undoubtedly been positive, but whether or not legislative and policy change should follow inquiries into the management of unique and complex cases is open to question. This chapter tracks some of the major policy shifts associated with key inquiries and reviews at different points from 1945 to 2007 and considers the extent to which inquiries and reviews lead to positive improvements in child protection policy and practice. Both Scottish and English inquiries and reviews have influenced child care and protection policy and practice in Scotland. This chapter, therefore, considers all UK inquiries and reviews that have had an important impact.

EARLY INQUIRIES AND DEVELOPMENT OF THE CHILD PROTECTION SYSTEM

The Denis O'Neill Inquiry in 1945 was the first inquiry in the UK relating to child abuse. Thirteen-year-old Denis died of cruelty and neglect while living with foster parents. The Denis O'Neill Inquiry had a direct influence on the development of policy to protect children. It was a major influence and impetus for obtaining support for the establishment of unified local authority Children's Departments and the 1948 Children Act which emphasised family preservation (Reder *et al.*, 1993; Reder and Duncan, 1996; Holman *et al.*, 1999; Butler and Drakeford, 2003). The 1948 Act was regarded as a major step forward for child welfare. Most of the Act's provisions applied to Scotland as well as England and Wales but the Denis O'Neill Inquiry did not lead to the same level of children's service developments in Scotland in the 1950s as it did in England and Wales. Abrams (1998) argues that it took until the 1960s before there was a comparable shift in child welfare services in Scotland. The *Glasgow Herald*, reporting on the Denis O'Neill case back in 1945, stated:

> Fortunately Scotland, as in most matters connected to the education and welfare of children, is much in advance of England, and there is little reason to fear that such things as have been called attention to in England could happen this side of the border. (cited in Sen *et al.*, 2007)

Yet Sen *et al.* (2007) point out that less than six months after the death of Denis O'Neill, foster carers John and Margaret Walton were convicted of wilful mistreatment of 12-year-old Norman and 10-year-old Harry Wilson in Fife.

Reporting in 1974 the Maria Colwell Inquiry had a huge impact on the child protection system across the whole of the UK. Maria was a seven-year-old girl who died after being beaten and neglected by her stepfather and mother. She had been returned home on a supervision order after having been placed with relative foster carers. The public inquiry into Maria's death generated considerable media interest in the issue of child abuse. It led to the introduction of Child Protection Registers and case conferences and prompted the 1975 Children Act and the introduction of Child Protection Committees (Munro, 2004; Reder and Duncan, 2004; Reder *et al.*, 1993; Corby *et al.*, 2001). Reder and Duncan (2004) have described the Maria Colwell Inquiry report in 1974 as a 'landmark event that fundamentally changed child protection practice'. In Scotland the Richard Clark Inquiry took place shortly after the Maria Colwell Inquiry and further emphasised the need for changes to the child protection system in Scotland.

INQUIRIES OF THE 1980S AND 1990S

The child's right to protection

Interestingly there were no public inquiries during the 1980s in Scotland (Galilee, 2005). There were, however, many in England and as a result child abuse remained on the public and political agenda throughout the decade in Scotland as well as in the rest of the UK. The inquiries of the 1980s had an important impact on professional practice. The Jasmine Beckford Inquiry in 1985 (London Borough of Brent, 1985) led to a rise in referrals and a

particularly sharp increase in the number of children placed on Child Protection Registers and/or made subject to Place of Safety Orders across the
UK, and increasing numbers of children were taken into care following the
Inquiry. In contrast to the 1970s when the state was reluctant to intervene
in family life, the child's right to protection assumed more prominence in
the 1980s, in terms of guiding social work practice, than family preservation
(Butler and Drakeford, 2003). Inquiry reports of the 1980s which concluded
that the needs and rights of parents should take second place to the primary
task of protecting children certainly played a key role in bringing about this
change in emphasis.

Inquiries into abuse in residential care

Prior to the 1990s inquiries focused on the physical abuse and/or neglect of
children at home by their parents or carers. Until then very few concerns
had been raised in relation to the abuse of children in other settings, and
no inquiries had focused on sexual abuse. In the late 1980s and early 1990s
there were a number of inquiries into abuse in residential homes in England
and one inquiry, the Edinburgh Inquiry, in Scotland. Some of these inquiries
identified widespread sexual abuse over many decades. They led to an acceptance among professionals and the public that institutional and sexual abuse
existed. A Scottish Office discussion document published in 1982 included a
reference to sexual abuse for the first time. However, a Government circular,
also dated 1982, setting out categories for possible registration of child abuse
listed only physical injury, physical neglect, failure to thrive and children at
risk; sexual abuse was not mentioned. It was not until 1992, a year after the
publication of the Orkney Inquiry, that a report setting out the categories
of abuse that should be used in recording and registering child abuse cases
included the category of sexual abuse (Black and Williams, 2002).

The inquiries into past abuse in residential care in the late 1980s and 1990s
also led to pressure on governments to review the quality of care for children
in residential units. The Utting report into residential care in England in 1991,
Children in the Public Care, and *Another Kind of Home*, a report examining the
quality of residential care in Scotland (Skinner, 1992), followed these inquiries
(Corby *et al.*, 2001). The Utting Report was a direct consequence of the 'Pindown' Report (Staffordshire County Council, 1991). 'Pindown' hit the head-
lines in 1991. The practice involved punishing children who had absconded
or who refused to attend school by confining them in a sparsely furnished
room and depriving them of possessions and company. The practice, which

was devised by and authorised by senior management, operated in Stafford-shire between 1983 and 1989. A television programme exposing the practice led to an Inquiry.

Abuse in residential care remained on the political agenda throughout the 1990s. The realisation that some staff in residential and foster care abused children and young people in their care led to the introduction of more rigorous selection processes. Scottish Criminal Records Office (SCRO) checks were undertaken for all residential staff and others with direct access to children from 1989. Following the inquiry into the Beck case in England the government commissioned the Warner report (1992) to investigate recruitment and selection processes for residential staff. In Scotland the Scottish Office commissioned the Kent Report (1997) to consider the dangers faced by children living away from home following the growing number of abuse cases in residential child care. The report made recommendations around complaints, vetting of staff, accountability of staff, retention of files, and monitoring.

Balancing the protection of children with the rights of parents

If most of the inquiries undertaken in the UK in the early 1980s focused on the need for professionals to intervene to protect children, by the end of the 1980s there was a change of emphasis. Inquiries such as Cleveland in England and Orkney in Scotland concluded that professionals had too much power and were intervening unnecessarily. In Cleveland 121 children were made the subject of emergency care orders within six months based on a controversial test for anal abuse (Secretary of State for Social Services, 1988). A major theme of the Cleveland Inquiry, like the Orkney Inquiry, was overzealous intrusion into family life. Both Inquiries challenged the existing child protection provisions of the 1968 Social Work (Scotland) Act and gave support to the Children Act (1989) and the Children (Scotland) Act 1995 with their new legal concept of parental responsibility. Both acts emphasised that children were best brought up by their birth family and that every effort should be made to keep the child in the family home. They stressed that professionals should work in partnership with parents and that removing children should be viewed as a last resort.

The Children (Scotland) Act 1995 introduced new criteria of 'significant harm' as the basis for intervention. It aimed to balance the protection of children with the rights of parents and ensure compulsory intervention was undertaken only where absolutely necessary. The introduction of the concept of significant harm, coupled with the concept of minimum intervention embodied in the 'no order' principle, potentially created a higher threshold for intervention than existed under the previous legislation (McGhee and Francis, 2003). New government guidelines in England and Wales in 1991 and Scottish Office guidance in 1998 also reflected the shift to working more cooperatively with parents involved in child protection procedures. The emphasis moved more in the direction of supporting families, rather than investigating them, and the Cleveland and Orkney Inquiries helped support this change (Munro, 2004; Corby *et al.*, 2001).

New emergency protection measures

Both the Orkney Report and the Cleveland Report reflected the growing concern around the need to establish legal guidelines for the urgent removal of children from their home in the interests of protecting them from harm, while at the same time recognising parental rights and responsibilities (Asquith, 1993). Following the Children (Scotland) Act 1995 courts were given a greater role in child protection decision making. Prior to the Act the main emergency route to protect children was to apply to a Justice of the Peace for a Place of Safety Order (Section 37(2) Social Work Scotland Act 1968). Excessive use of Place of Safety Orders had been a primary focus of examination in the Cleveland report. The Place of Safety Order was also criticised in the Orkney Inquiry report. The authors of the Orkney report concluded that the scope of discretion allowed in relation to the grounds for removal was excessive and ran counter to Article 8 of the European Convention on Human Rights, the 'right to respect for family life'. The Inquiry recommended that Section 37 (2) of the Social Work (Scotland) Act 1968 be rewritten so a child could only be removed where he or she was likely to suffer imminent and significant harm and where removal was necessary for his or her protection. It also recommended that the child and his or her parent should have an immediate opportunity to have the order varied or cancelled by the sheriff. These recommendations directly influenced the development of the Child Protection Order within the Children (Scotland) Act 1995 (McGhee and Francis, 2003; Asquith, 1993). Child Protection Orders (CPOs) replaced Place of Safety Orders in the 1995 Act. CPOs allowed for the detention or retention of a child in a place of safety for up to eight days where there was risk of significant harm. Clear criteria for the order and for making a legal challenge against it were set out. Parents (and other adults in certain cases) and children had the right to apply for the recall or variation of a CPO once during the eight-day period following the implementation of the order.

Following the Orkney Inquiry there was a downward trend in the use of emergency protection measures to remove or detain a child in a place of safety (McGhee and Francis, 2003). This trend continued following the 1995 Act demonstrating that the Orkney Inquiry had an important impact on child protection practice. The new emergency protection orders introduced under the 1995 Act were more accountable and balanced the rights of parents with those of children. The CPO was a fairer process for parents and children but in practice very few parents exercised the right to apply to recall or vary the order. There were only 52 applications to recall and five to vary a CPO up to December 1999, leading McGhee and Francis (2003) to question:

> whether the new provisions have resulted in more effective methods of safeguarding the welfare of children or if the threshold of risk has potentially risen to a level that is resulting in circumstances where, previously, urgent action may have been taken.

More recent inquiries and reviews, for example the review into the abuse of children in Eilean Siar, have concluded that children should have been removed much earlier and suggest that McGhee and Francis are right. The many parallels between the recent Eilean Siar case and the Richard Clark case back in 1975 suggest that the 1995 Act may not have had the impact that was intended. This begs the question of whether legislative change should be made on the back of inquiry recommendations.

Children's rights

Inquiry reports have influenced policy and practice in relation to children's rights. Nearly all inquiries have concluded that listening to children is of key importance if we are to identify and tackle child abuse. Many of the inquiry reports of the 1990s highlighted the need to safeguard the rights of children. The Orkney Inquiry report highlighted the importance of listening to children. It recommended an enhancement of the role of the safeguarder to represent the needs and interests of the child. The Orkney Inquiry was also influential in the formulation of the Memorandum of good practice for interviewing children (Corby and Cox, 2000).

The North Wales Tribunal report (Waterhouse, 2000) recommended the appointment of a Children's Commissioner for Wales and made a number of recommendations regarding complaints procedures (Corby et al., 2001). The Edinburgh Inquiry raised at national level the need for a Scotland-wide Children's Commissioner. It also made many other recommendations relating to children's rights, including some relating to complaints.

In response to the recommendations from these inquiries the Children (Scotland) Act 1995 brought conformity with the UN Convention on the Rights of the Child and ensured children would be involved in decision making. It also promoted the development of individual care planning for young people who were looked after.

Measures to protect children in the community

The Inquiry into the events at Dunblane in 1996 had an impact on policy relating to the licensing and use of firearms. The Inquiry did not recommend the banning of handguns but made recommendations for alterations to the licensing and use of handguns. The Conservative Government went further than the recommendations in the report, introducing the Firearms (Amendment) Act 1997 that brought about a ban on private ownership of high calibre handguns (above .22) and restrictions on the use of others. The subsequent Labour Government then brought in the Firearms (Amendment) (No. 2) Act 1997 that outlawed remaining handguns, with a few exceptions.

Prior to Dunblane there was little if any published guidance on tackling the dangers that an unauthorised intruder could pose to the pupils and teachers in schools. In the aftermath of Dunblane there were calls for additional measures to protect the school population. The Inquiry undoubtedly had a substantial impact in terms of raising awareness of this issue. The findings of the Dunblane Inquiry also led to proposals to vet and supervise adults working with children and young people. Before Dunblane there was no coherent system in place for vetting people like Thomas Hamilton who operated clubs, or for monitoring their conduct. Dunblane was a catalyst for development of policy in this area. Further policy changes have been made, in part at least, in relation to more recent inquiries such as the Bichard Inquiry that inquired into events in Soham.

INQUIRIES AND REVIEWS IN THE 21ST CENTURY

The national audit and review of child protection in Scotland

The Kennedy McFarlane Inquiry was particularly influential in Scotland this century. The Inquiry report recommended that there should be an audit of child protection processes across Scotland to look at the consistency and quality of practice from individual agencies and from agencies working together. On the back of this recommendation Jack McConnell (then Minister for Education, Europe and External Affairs) ordered an audit and review of child protection across Scotland. The review aimed to promote the reduction of abuse or neglect of children and to improve the services for children who experience abuse or neglect. *It's Everyone's Job to Make Sure I'm Alright*, the Report of the Child Protection Audit and Review, was published in November 2002 and made 17 recommendations.

The Child Protection Reform Programme

The Scottish Executive's response to *It's Everyone's Job to Make Sure I'm Alright* was a five-point action plan that included the setting up of a three-year child protection reform programme which had a wider remit than responding to the specific recommendations in the review. There were a number of outputs from the programme:

- a Children's Charter;
- a Framework for Standards;
- Guidance for Child Protection Committees;
- Multi-agency Inspection;
- a public awareness campaign;
- a 24-hour single national helpline number;
- letters of assurance (seeking assurance that local authorities, health boards and police authorities were reviewing child protection arrangements, had established action plans and had robust quality assurance arrangements in place);
- Guidance for Significant Case Reviews;
- a multi-agency training framework and a national suite of materials to support the framework.

In a sense this whole national programme of work stemmed from the Kennedy McFarlane Inquiry report. The reform programme took forward many of the recommendations of the Kennedy McFarlane report as well as many of the recommendations from more recent reviews that reported during the period of the reform programme.

The Carla Nicole Bone and Danielle Reid review reports both recommended a central help line and a leaflet for the public and both of these recommendations were taken forward under the reform programme. A number of professionals who were interviewed in Scotland for the Process Review of the Child Protection Reform Programme (Daniel *et al.*, 2007) attributed a rise in public awareness to high profile cases involving child deaths and serious abuse and neglect that were reported in the media during the lifespan of the reform programme.

Many of the recommendations around accountability in recent inquiry and review reports were taken forward under the reform programme in the form of guidance to Child Protection Committees and new multi-agency inspection processes. Letters of assurance to chief executives of local authorities and health boards and chief constables also improved accountability by ensuring that child protection was placed on the agenda at the most senior levels within agencies and organisations (Daniel *et al.*, 2007).

The work around training in the reform programme took account of recent inquiries, most notably the Caleb Ness Inquiry, which found that criminal justice and community care social workers had had no training in child protection and did not believe they had any responsibility for child protection. Children at the Centre, a project funded by the Scottish Executive to train criminal justice and community care social workers in child protection, alongside child and family social workers, was completed in March 2007. Nearly 3000 social workers from all the local authorities in Scotland were trained under the programme (Daniel *et al.*, 2007).

Agencies have become far more alert to the issue of parental substance misuse as a result of the Caleb Ness Inquiry report as well as other high profile incidents connected with parental substance misuse that did not result in public inquiries, for example, the death of Michael McGarrity's mother and the death of Derek Doran from methadone ingestion. The links between child protection and substance misuse have been more clearly identified. The Caleb Ness Inquiry directly led to the second letter of assurance which asked local authorities, health authorities and police forces to assure ministers that they were acting in response to parental substance misuse. Clearer protocols around drug use in pregnancy and neonatal withdrawal have been introduced as a result of the Caleb Ness Inquiry, Scottish Training on Drugs and Alcohol (STRADA) and Dundee University have provided training on child protection with a focus on substance-misusing parents and Drug Action Teams (DATs) and Child Protection Committees (CPCs) have developed far more joint strategies and procedures (Stafford and Vincent, 2008).

Scottish inquiry and review reports have also had an impact on policy in relation to the management of sex offenders. The Colyn Evans report led to changes in the management of sex offenders. The case highlighted the difficulties of managing a young person displaying sexually problematic or aggressive behaviour safely in an open residential setting. The authors of the report recommended that discussions should take place with a view to developing a national strategy for meeting the needs of young people displaying this type of behaviour. Many of the problems around the management of Colyn Evans occurred because Colyn was not a registered sex offender. The Management of Sex Offenders (Scotland) Bill 2005 introduced a legislative basis for agencies to work together to assess and manage not only registered sex offenders but other individuals considered to pose a danger to the public. The Violent and Sex Offenders Register (Visor) system now enables the electronic management of registered and non-registered sex offenders and some non-registered sex offenders have been brought into new risk assessment and management arrangements. Juvenile offenders, such as Colyn, who are dealt with through the Children's Hearing system remain, however, outside the terms of the legislation. Colyn Evans could not be required to register as a sex offender because he was dealt with by the hearing system. Neither the police nor social work could apply for a Sex Offender Prevention order in this case as Colyn had no sexual conviction as such because he was a juvenile.

The Victoria Climbie Inquiry

The Victoria Climbie Inquiry report has been particularly significant in shaping child care and protection policy in Scotland as well as in the rest of the UK. The Victoria Climbie Inquiry was a catalyst for introducing an integrated service delivery structure within the overarching policy of Every Child Matters in England (Parton, 2004). New legislation in the form of the Children Act 2004 reflected an attempt to transform the entire culture of children's services. The emphasis became one of providing preventive services for all children through safeguarding rather than protection to ensure earlier identification of additional needs and earlier intervention and service provision. Safeguarding applies to all the problems that may disrupt a child's health and development, not just abuse and neglect (Munro and Calder, 2005). The Victoria Climbie Inquiry took place at the same time as the National Audit and Review of Child Protection in Scotland and the recommendations of this inquiry informed the work of the audit and review team and also informed the subsequent Child Protection Reform Programme.

Getting it Right for Every Child (GIRFEC)

Getting it Right for Every Child (GIRFEC) is a new approach to children's policy in Scotland. It has been informed by the findings of the Victoria Climbie Inquiry as well as the findings of recent inquiries and reviews in Scotland. Getting It Right for Every Child does not directly refer to 'safeguarding' but, as in England, the emphasis is on meeting the needs of all children. The GIRFEC reforms address many of the practice themes identified in inquiries and reviews that were outlined in Chapter 5. A new assessment framework addresses many of the issues around assessment and aims to ensure that professionals take account of the child, family and environmental themes identified in Chapter 4. The GIRFEC reforms are accompanied by new information-sharing protocols designed to address many of the problems around communication that have been identified in inquiries and reviews.

Although the GIRFEC reforms take account of the findings of recent inquiries and reviews they did not result directly from one inquiry or review. The Child Protection Reform Programme had already taken forward many of the recommendations of recent inquiries and reviews and the GIRFEC reforms have built on this substantial programme of work. GIRFEC has been introduced slowly and without new legislation. The Scottish Government are committed to learning the lessons from pathfinder projects before implementing the GIRFEC approach across Scotland and there appears to be a genuine commitment to cultural change as opposed to purely structural change. It is, however, too early to say whether GIRFEC will be able to address all of the themes identified in inquiries and reviews, particularly those associated with anomalies of the Children (Scotland) Act 1995 which may yet need legislative change if they are to be fully addressed.

Regulation of care services

In 2007 the Scottish Government and Glasgow City Council commissioned an inquiry into abuse over a number of years at Kerelaw Residential School and Secure Unit. The Inquiry investigated historical and more recent abuse and concluded that abuse continued to take place after 1996 and into this century. In addition to the Children (Scotland) Act 1995 there was a further important legislative development in Scotland this century which responded to some of the recommendations of earlier inquiries into abuse in residential care such as the Edinburgh and Fife inquiries. The Regulation of Care (Scotland) Act 2001 created the Scottish Commission for the Regulation of Care (The Care Commission), an independent body charged with the regulation and inspection of care services. Before the Act child care services were subject to a range of different regulations: private and voluntary sector residential care homes were regulated by local authorities and secure accommodation was regulated by the Social Work Services Inspectorate (SWSI); local authority-run homes were not subject to registration at all. The Act also established the Scottish Social Services Council (SSSC) as the registration body with responsibility for setting standards for qualifications and behaviour of care workers, and all residential care workers are required to register by September 2009. It is disturbing that abuse in residential care continued to occur this century. The author of the Kerelaw report sheds some light on why these new legislative developments may not have protected young people at Kerelaw. He comments that most of the factors that contributed to what went wrong at Kerelaw have been identified in previous inquiries in Scotland and elsewhere. His investigation looked at whether the findings and recommendations from previous inquiries had been considered, and where appropriate, implemented. He concluded that Glasgow City Council was aware of the recommendations of the Edinburgh and Fife inquiries, as well as the recommendations of other inquiries in England, and considered the implications of these recommendations for their own services. Although Glasgow City Council took account of the lessons from these inquiries he concluded, however, that they appeared to have had little impact on practice in Kerelaw because ' there appears to have been a culture which made Kerelaw less well placed than it might have been to adapt to new legislative and policy requirements' (Frizzell, 2009, p. 50).

Frizzell (2009) suggests that strategies and policies are insufficient in themselves to effect change and adequately safeguard young people:

> The main failings at Kerelaw were not so much to do with legislation, policies or procedures, of which there was no shortage, as with people failing to comply with those procedures, failing to give leadership and direction, failing to deal with difficult management issues of which they were aware, and failing to care as they should have about disadvantaged, difficult and vulnerable young people with whose welfare they were entrusted. (p. 143)

POSITIVE OR NEGATIVE IMPACT?

Asquith (1993) stated that it is perhaps a sad comment on developments in child protection that legislative change has usually followed events in which children have been the victims of appalling injuries, often resulting in their death. Some of the policy and practice changes which have resulted from implementing the recommendations of inquiry reports and reviews have undoubtedly been positive and have contributed to raised awareness of child abuse, development of better inter-agency systems, and improved cooperation and communication. Improvements in staff selection and recruitment, in responding to allegations of abuse, in policies around whistle-blowing, monitoring and inspection, and around the promotion of children's rights have been cited as particularly positive impacts (Corby *et al.*, 2001).

The idea of single cases influencing radical change of legislation and policy has, however, been questioned and there are certainly questions to be raised about the effectiveness of legislative and policy change introduced following unique and complex cases. Changes resulting from major inquiries and reviews may not always be positive. Munro (2004) suggests that change brought about by the Victoria Climbie and other inquiries has been largely structural. While inquiries and reviews may have resulted in clearer lines of accountability and closer monitoring to ensure compliance, Munro argues that these types of structural change do not necessarily bring about improvements in quality. She suggests that the fact that some of the practice highlighted in the Victoria Climbie case was so poor may be evidence that new procedures introduced to improve practice on the back of previous inquiries were not successful.

There is undoubtedly learning to be gained from the detailed scrutiny of major, complex and tragic cases; indeed it would be negligent not to learn from such cases. There is, however, a debate to be had about whether tragic deaths have had an inordinate and inappropriate level of influence on policy to protect children (Parton, 2004; Masson, 2006) and whether a parallel approach to policy change and development based on learning from the everyday practices and successes of professionals working with vulnerable children, might be of equal value.

CONCLUSION

This chapter tracked some of the major policy shifts associated with key inquiries and reviews in Scotland and elsewhere in the UK and considered the extent to which inquiries and reviews have lead to positive improvements in child protection policy and practice. The main findings are that:

❑ Early inquiries influenced the development of the child protection system as we now know it.

❑ A number of influential inquiries in the 1980s gave support to the principles behind new legislation which sought to clarify the role of the state in the protection of children and outlined the relationship between professionals and parents in ensuring the welfare of children.

❑ While earlier inquiries focused on the abuse of children at home by their parents, in the 1990s there were a number of inquiries into past and recent abuse of children in other settings, for example in residential children's homes. Inquiries in the late 1980s and 1990s led to more acceptance of the phenomenon of child sexual abuse, put pressure on policy makers to improve the safety and quality of care for children and young people in the care system, and emphasised the importance of the concept of children's rights.

❑ Dunblane and other high profile inquiries highlighted new issues around community safety and resulted in legislative and policy change.

❑ In the 21st century, reform of the child protection system in Scotland was introduced following the Kennedy McFarlane case. The Child Protection Reform Programme attempted to address findings from the Kennedy McFarlane case as well as findings from a number of inquiries and reviews which reported during the time the reform programme was underway.

❑ 'Getting it Right for Every Child' addresses many of the issues raised by inquiries and reviews.

❑ Child deaths and abuse and neglect have continued to occur despite significant legislative and policy developments, and the extent to which good policy and legislation is made in the wake of unique and complex cases is worthy of further discussion.

The final chapter, Chapter 7, looks at what we can learn from cases of child death and serious abuse in Scotland.

CHAPTER 7

Conclusion: Learning from child death and abuse cases

The main focus of this book is to explore what we can learn from cases of child death and significant abuse in Scotland. Chapter 1 set the scene by looking at numbers of child deaths and considering what proportion of deaths are caused by abuse and neglect. Chapter 2 outlined the processes that are used to inquire into and review cases of child death or other significant cases in Scotland as well as in other parts of the UK. Chapter 3 identified key public inquiries and reviews into child death and child abuse in Scotland and the following two chapters identified the main themes from these inquiries and reviews. Chapter 4 looked at child, family and environmental themes and agency themes were discussed in Chapter 5. Chapter 6 considered what impact major inquiries and reviews have had on child protection policy and practice.

There have been no national analyses of Significant Case Reviews in Scotland as there have of Serious Case Reviews in England and Wales. Scottish evidence is, therefore, limited to the small number of publicly available inquiries and reviews that have been discussed in this book. It would be difficult to arrive at firm conclusions about the main themes from such a small number of cases. For this reason Chapters 4 and 5 also presented evidence from inquiries and reviews in England and Wales and pointed to similarities and differences between the findings in Scotland and those identified elsewhere.

While Chapter 4 identified a number of child, family and environmental themes that professionals working with children and families in Scotland should take into account, it is important to remember that most cases of serious harm will be unpredictable. The majority of children living with high levels of adversity will not be experiencing serious abuse and overreaction can be dangerous. The child, family and environmental themes identified in Chapter 4 may be seen as potential risk factors, but these individual risk factors may not be significant when considered in isolation. Instead, the evidence from Scotland and elsewhere (Brandon *et al.*, 2008; Ofsted, 2008a; Rose and Barnes, 2008) suggests that the families of children who die or suffer significant abuse experience multiple difficulties and it is the coexistence of several risk factors, and the way in which these various risk factors interact, which is important in terms of predicting death and abuse.

Evidence from inquiries and reviews in Scotland suggests that very young children may be particularly vulnerable. This concurs with findings from England and Wales and from international homicide studies. Because the findings from Significant Case Reviews have not been collated in Scotland it is not possible to say whether there has been an increase in cases involving hard-to-help teenagers as there has been in England and Wales. Only one of the Scottish inquiries and reviews considered in this book, the Colyn Evans review, related to a teenager.

Children with disabilities or health or behavioural problems may also be at higher risk of death or abuse. Certainly parents of babies with disabilities or health needs may require significant levels of support if they are to be able to provide satisfactory levels of care and protection for their children, particularly when they are vulnerable themselves.

Evidence from inquiries and reviews suggests that children in Scotland are at more risk from men than women, both at home as well as in the community, including residential care settings. It is essential that safe care and parenting programmes are aimed at fathers and male carers as well as mothers and the parenting/caring abilities of fathers and significant males should be given more weight in assessment. Women who are experiencing domestic abuse may find it difficult to protect their children. All professionals working with children and families should be aware of the link between domestic abuse and risk of harm to children and need to consider the risk that significant males may pose to vulnerable women and children. Unfortunately professionals are not always aware that violent males are living in households with children until after the significant incident occurs. Professionals need to be able to find out who is living in households with children and to find ways of tracking violent adults who may be a significant danger to children. Many of the men who have harmed children have been found to have criminal records, often for violent offences. The police may hold important information relating to criminal convictions or suspected criminal activity which should be included in assessing the risks adults pose to children.

Substance misuse, mental health issues, learning disabilities and other health difficulties may also impact on a parent or carer's capacity to care for and protect their child and should be taken into account in assessments of risk and need. In families where more than one of these factors is found, or one or more of these factors exists in combination with domestic abuse, the risk may be high, particularly to very young babies.

Environmental factors such as poverty, housing problems or lack of social support can be significant stress factors for families. On its own poverty is unlikely to be a predictor of child death or significant abuse but, as Brandon *et al.* (2002) have pointed out, poverty may form a backdrop to other factors likely to impede parents' capacity to protect their children, and professionals should consider the implications of poverty and financial problems in families where parenting problems have already been identified. Housing may be the first agency to have contact with a child. Housing workers should, therefore, be alert to signs of abuse and neglect and know what to do if they have concerns about a child. Where families move home frequently this may be an indicator that something is wrong. Changes of address may indicate that families are attempting to avoid contact by agencies. Agencies need to be able to maintain contact with families when they move and minimise disruptions to service provision following moves.

Practitioners need to obtain as much information about parents' and carers' own childhoods as they can and include this information in assessing their caretaking abilities and ability to protect their children. Historical information, about the ways in which parents looked after other children, particularly children who may now be in care, may be significant and should be taken into account when assessing risk and need and assessing parenting skills.

Patterns of help-seeking can be warning signs of parenting difficulties and abuse, for example frequent admissions to accident and emergency, a history of injuries or a history of illness. Changes from cooperation to non-cooperation of families may also be significant. If families no longer welcome visits this may be an indicator that something is wrong. Evidence from inquiries and reviews also suggests that professionals should be alert to the fact that abusive parents may be, or appear to be, loving parents.

In order to adequately assess the risks to children professionals need extensive training in and appreciation of child development and attachment theory, as well as training in key knowledge concerning factors such as substance misuse, mental illness and domestic abuse. Evidence from inquiries and reviews also suggests that professionals in all agencies require training in basic skills in communicating with children to ensure that practice is child centred. Practitioners need to ensure they see and speak to children and should be alert to the fact that children may try to report abuse in very subtle ways. When there is insufficient evidence of demonstrable change in a child's circumstances and well-being, agencies may need to act to protect a child. Practitioners may need significant levels of support to work with hostile and aggressive parents and supervision should include supporting practitioners to cope with the emotional demands of work with children and families as well as checking and accountability.

Assessment frameworks can help professionals consider all the risk factors in a child's life. They can also help them identify potential strengths and supports in children's lives that may protect them from risks. Evidence from inquiries and reviews suggest, however, that risk needs to be managed as well as assessed. Risk assessments are only one tool to assess the risk an abuser is likely to present to children. They must form part of a wider assessment of a child's needs for care and protection, together with an assessment of the ability of the non-abusing partner to protect them. It is also important to remember that levels of risk may change at any time and that risk assessment is an ongoing process, not simply a one-off exercise.

Inquiries and reviews have shown that children who are at serious risk of harm may not always be found within formal child protection systems. The most vulnerable children may be those on the margins of the child protection system. These children and their families may have minimal involvement with agencies. Families do not have to engage with services unless thresholds of significant harm are reached and agencies may need to consider more effective, creative ways of engaging some of these young people and families. If a family fails to accept or take up a service this should be taken into account in assessment and it may raise the level of concern to one where child protection procedures need to be instigated. Where children are not within the formal child protection system staff in universal services play a key role in keeping them safe and it is vitally important that they have the necessary skills and knowledge to identify and respond to signs of abuse. Poor attendance at school may be an indicator of child protection issues and should always be investigated. Missed health appointments may be another warning sign.

While inquiries and reviews may be useful in enabling us to identify warning signs in other families, the extent to which they are a useful vehicle for generating lessons to be learned has been questioned. We need to remember, as Rose and Barnes (2008) point out, that child deaths and cases of significant abuse are rare and the majority of children are protected by universal services and child protection agencies. Inquiries and reviews are only one source of evidence about what is happening in child protection work and cases where things have gone wrong should be set alongside the numbers of children who are being protected at any one time. Rose and Barnes (2008) conclude that learning from effective safeguarding practice rather than from mistakes might, therefore, be a more effective way of learning. They acknowledge, however, that learning from what works well would require a major shift in a country where child protection policy and practice has traditionally focused on what has gone wrong.

Chapter 1 provided evidence from other countries which suggests that a public health approach where we can look at preventing all deaths, rather than just those that are known to be the result of abuse and neglect, might be a more effective way of learning. In Chapter 2 we saw that some parts of the UK are moving in this direction and introducing processes to enable learning from review of all child deaths. It is too early to evaluate the success of these new processes but if our overall aim is to reduce the number of child deaths and cases of serious abuse then a preventative approach encompassing public health measures and public awareness campaigns may offer a way forward. A public health approach would enable the main risk factors associated with abuse and neglect discussed in this book, such as domestic abuse, mental health issues and substance misuse, to be addressed by targeting whole populations. Such an approach is particularly helpful because it enables attitudes to be changed in a non-stigmatising way. Universal services are able to identify vulnerable families at an early stage and intervene to change risky behaviours and thus avoid pathways to abuse and neglect (O'Donnell *et al.*, 2008).

While a public health approach has considerable appeal it may be difficult to implement in Scotland and the rest of the UK. We saw in Chapter 6 the significant impact that inquiries and reviews into individual cases of child death and serious abuse have had on child care and protection policy and practice. To a large extent the impact has been so great because we have a forensically driven, risk-averse child protection system and a 'culture of blame' when things go wrong (Franklin, 1999; Franklin and Parton, 2001; Parton, 1996). Within such a culture it may be very difficult to move away from a learning approach that focuses on identifying risks in individual cases where things have gone wrong towards a public health approach where the emphasis is on the prevention of all risks that may impair well-being and development. In Scotland new child care policy developments such as GIRFEC certainly offer the potential to move towards a public health approach. GIRFEC aims to promote safe, healthy development for all children, not just those who are suffering or are at risk of suffering harm, and universal, targeted and specialist services all have a role to play in meeting their needs for care and protection. GIRFEC sits, however, alongside a well-established child protection system that retains most of its forensic, investigative aspects and it will be interesting to see whether the GIRFEC principles which coalesce with a public health approach will bring about a shift in the culture of children's services in Scotland.

References

Abrams, L. (1998) *The Orphan Country: Children of Scotland's Broken Homes from 1845 to the Present Day*, Edinburgh: John Donald

Arthurs, Y. and Ruddick, J. (2001) *An Analysis of Child Protection 'Part 8' Reviews Carried Out over a Two Year Period in the South East Region of the NHS*, London: Department of Health

Asquith, S. (1993) *Protecting Children: Cleveland to Orkney: More Lessons to Learn?* Edinburgh: HMSO

Axford, N. and Bullock, R. (2005) *Child Death and Significant Case Reviews: International Approaches*, Edinburgh: Scottish Executive

Barnard, M. (2007) *Drug Addiction and Families*, London: Jessica Kingsley

Bell, N. (2007) 'Children's residential services: learning through records', in Shaw, T. (2007) *Historical Abuse Systemic Review*, Edinburgh: Scottish Government

Berridge, D. and Brodie, I. (1996) 'Residential child care in England and Wales: the inquiries and after', in Hill, M. and Aldgate, J. (eds) (1996) *Child Welfare Services: Developments in Law, Policy, Practice and Research*, London: Jessica Kingsley

Black, A. and Williams, C. (2002) *Fife Council Independent Enquiry Established by the Chief Executive Following the Conviction of David Logan Murphy for the Sexual Abuse of Children*, Kirkcaldy: Fife Council

Brandon, M., Howe, D., Black, J. and Dodsworth, J. (2002) *Learning How to Make Children Safer Part 2: An Analysis for the Welsh Office of Serious Child Abuse Cases in Wales*, University of East Anglia/Welsh Office

Brandon, M., Dodsworth, J. and Rumball, D. (2005) 'Serious Case Reviews: learning to use expertise', *Child Abuse Review*, Vol. 14, No. 3, pp. 160–76

Brandon, M., Belderson, P., Warren, C., Howe, D., Gardner, R., Dodsworth, J. and Black, J. (2008) *Analysing Child Deaths and Serious Injury through Abuse and Neglect: What Can We Learn?*, Department for Children, Schools and Families

Brandon, M., Bailey, S., Belderson, P., Gardner, R., Sidebotham, P., Dodsworth, J., Warren, C. and Black, J. (2009) *Understanding Serious Case Reviews and their Impact*, London: Department for Children, Schools and Families

Bunting, L. and Reid, C. (2005) 'Reviewing child deaths – learning from the American experience', *Child Abuse Review*, Vol. 14, No. 2, pp. 82–96

Butler, I. and Drakeford, M. (2003) *Social Policy, Social Welfare and Scandal: How British Public Policy is Made*, Basingstoke: Palgrave Macmillan

CEMACH (2008) *Perinatal Mortality 2006: England, Wales and Northern Ireland*, London: CEMACH

Cleaver, H., Unell, I. and Aldgate, J. (1999) *Children's needs – Parenting capacity: the Impact of Parental Mental Illness, Problem Alcohol and Drug Use and Domestic Violence on Children's Development*, London: Stationery Office

Cleaver, H., Nicholson, D., Tarr, S. and Cleaver, D. (2007) *Child Protection, Domestic Violence and Parental Substance Misuse*, London: Jessica Kingsley

Clyde, J. J. (1992) *The Report of the Inquiry into the Removal of Children from Orkney in February 1991*, Edinburgh: HMSO

Colton, M. (2002) 'Factors associated with abuse in residential child care institutions', *Children and Society*, Vol. 16, No. 1, pp. 33–44

Cooper, A. (2005) 'Surface and depth in the Victoria Climbie Inquiry Report', *Child and Family Social Work*, Vol. 10, No. 1, pp. 1–9

Corby, B. (2003) 'Towards a new means of inquiry into child abuse cases', *Journal of Social Welfare and Family Law*, Vol. 25, No. 3, pp. 229–41

Corby, B. and Cox, P. (2000) 'Using child abuse inquiries in child protection education and training', *Social Work Education*, Vol. 19, No. 3, pp. 219–30

Corby, B., Doig, A. and Roberts, V. (2001) *Public Inquiries into Abuse of Children in Residential Care*, London: Jessica Kingsley

Craig, M. (2009) 'Safeguarding children who live with parental substance misuse', in Hughes, L. and Owen, H. (2009) *Good Practice in Safeguarding Children*, London: Jessica Kingsley

Creighton, S. (2001) 'Childhood deaths reported to coroners: an investigation of the contribution of abuse and neglect', in *Out of Sight, NSPCC Report on Child Abuse Deaths from Abuse 1973–2000*, London: NSPCC

Cullen, Lord (1996) *The Public Inquiry into the Shootings at Dunblane Primary School on 13 March 1996*, London: The Stationery Office

Daniel, B., Vincent, S. and Ogilvie-Whyte, S. (2007) *A Process Review of the Child Protection Reform Programme*, Edinburgh: Scottish Executive

Department for Education and Skills (2006), *Local Safeguarding Children Boards: A Review of Progress*, DfES

Department of Health (1991a) *Child Abuse: A Study of Inquiry Reports 1980–1989*, London: HMSO

Department of Health (1991b) *Working Together under the Children Act 1989*, London: HMSO

Department of Health and Social Security (1982) *Child Abuse: A Study of Inquiry Reports 1973–1981*, London: HMSO

Department of Health, Social Services and Public Safety (2003) *Co-operating to Safeguard Children*, Belfast: DHSSPS

Department of Health/Welsh Office (1988) *Working Together: A Guide to Arrangements for Inter-agency Co-operation for the Protection of Children from Abuse*, London: HMSO

Durfee, M., Tilton Durfee, D. and West, M. P. (2002) 'Child fatality review: an international movement', *Child Abuse and Neglect*, Vol. 26, pp. 619–36

Falkov, A. (1996) *A Study of Working Together Part 8 Reports: Fatal Child Abuse and Parental Psychiatric Disorder*, London: Department of Health

Fish, S., Munro, E. and Bairstow, S. (2008) *Learning Together to Safeguard Children: Developing a Multi-agency Approach for Case Reviews*, London: Social Care Institute for Excellence

Fleming, P. J., Blair, P., Bacon, C. and Berry, P. J. (eds) (2000) *Sudden Unexpected Deaths in Infancy: the CESDI SUDI Studies 1993–1996*, London: The Stationery Office

Franklin, B. (ed.) (1999) *Social Policy, the Media and Misrepresentation*, London: Routledge

Franklin, B. and Parton, N. (2001) 'Press-ganged! Media reporting of social work and child abuse', in May, M., Brunsden, E. and Page, R. (eds) *Understanding Social Problems: Issues in Social Policy*, Oxford: Blackwell

Frizzell, E. (2009) *Independent Inquiry into Abuse at Kerelaw Residential School and Secure Unit*, Edinburgh: Scottish Government

Galilee, J. (2005) *Learning from Failure: A Review of Major Social Care/Health Inquiry Recommendations*, Scottish Executive

Gilbert, R., Spatz Widom, C., Browne, K., Fergusson, D., Webb, E. and Janson, S. (2009) 'Burden and consequences of child maltreatment in high-income countries', *The Lancet*, Vol. 373, No. 9657, pp. 68–81

Hallett, C. (1989) 'Child abuse inquiries and public policy', in Stevenson, O. (ed.) (1989) *Child Abuse: Professional Practice and Public Policy*, London: Harvester Wheatsheaf

Hammond, H. (2001) *Child Protection Inquiry into the Circumstances Surrounding the Death of Kennedy McFarlane, d.o.b. 17 April 1997*, Dumfries: Dumfries and Galloway Child Protection Committee

Herbison, J. (2005) Danielle Reid: Independent Review into the Circumstances Surrounding her Death

HM Government (2006) *Working Together to Safeguard Children*, London: TSO

Hobbs, C. J., Wynne, J. and Gelletlie, R. (1995) 'Leeds inquiry into infant deaths: the importance of abuse and neglect in sudden infant death', *Child Abuse Review*, Vol. 4, pp. 329–39

Holman, B., Parker, R. and Utting, W. (1999) *Reshaping Childcare Practice*, London: National Institute for Social Work

Hughes, L. (2009) 'Making the most of a home visit', in Hughes, L. and Owen, H. (2009) *Good Practice in Safeguarding Children*, London: Jessica Kingsley

Jakob, R. and Gumbrell, G. (2009) 'Neglect and parental learning disability', in Hughes, L. and Owen, H. (2009) *Good Practice in Safeguarding Children*, London: Jessica Kingsley

James, G. (1994) *Study of Working Together Part 8 Reports*, London: Department of Health

Jenny, C. and Isaac, R (2006) 'The relation between child death and child maltreatment', *Archives of Disease in Childhood*, Vol. 91, No. 3, pp. 265–69

Jones, D. P. H., Hindley, N. and Ramchandani, P. (2006) 'Making plans: assessment, intervention and evaluating outcomes, in Aldgate, J., Jones, D. P. H. and Jeffery, C. (eds) (2006) *The Developing World of the Child*, London: Jessica Kingsley

Kent, R. (1997) *Children's Safeguards Review*, Edinburgh: HMSO

Kroll, B. and Taylor, A. (2003) *Parental Substance Misuse and Child Welfare*, London: Jessica Kingsley

Laming, Lord (2003) *The Victoria Climbie Inquiry Report, Cm 5730*, London: The Stationery Office

Levene, S. and Bacon, C. J. (2004) 'Sudden unexpected death and covert homicide in infancy', *Archives of Disease in Childhood*, Vol. 89, pp. 443–7

London Borough of Brent (1985) *A Child in Trust: the Report of the Panel of Inquiry into the Circumstances Surrounding the Death of Jasmine Beckford*, Middlesex: London Borough of Brent

Marshall, K., Jamieson, K. and Finlayson, A. (1999) *Edinburgh's Children: The Report of the Edinburgh Inquiry into Abuse and Protection of Children in Care*, City of Edinburgh Council

Masson, J. (2006) 'The Climbie Inquiry – context and critique', *Journal of Law and Society*, Vol. 33, No. 2, pp. 221–43

McGhee, J. and Francis, J. (2003) 'Protecting children in Scotland: examining the impact of the Children (Scotland) Act 1995', *Child and Family Social Work*, Vol. 8, pp. 133–42

Moore, A. (2005) 'Changing patterns of childhood mortality in Wolverhampton', *Archives of Disease in Childhood*, Vol. 90, pp. 687–91

Morris, L., Williams, L. and Beak, K. (2007) *A Study of Case Reviews Submitted to the Welsh Assembly Government under Chapter 8 of 'Working Together to Safeguard Children: a Guide to Interagency Working to Safeguard and Promote the Welfare of Children'*, Cardiff: University of Wales, Newport/National Assembly for Wales

Morrison, T. (1990) 'The emotional effects of child protection on the worker', *Practice*, Vol. 4, No. 4

Munro, E. (1999) 'Common errors of reasoning in child protection work', *Child Abuse and Neglect*, Vol. 23, No. 8, pp. 745–58

Munro, E. (2004) 'The impact of child abuse inquiries since 1990', in Stanley, N. and Manthorpe, J. (eds) (2004) *The Age of the Inquiry: Learning and Blaming in Health and Social Care*, London: Routledge

Munro, E. (2005) 'What tools do we need to improve identification of child abuse?', *Child Abuse Review*, Vol. 14, pp. 374–88

Munro, E. and Calder, M. C. (2005) 'Where has child protection gone?', *Political Quarterly*, Vol. 76, No. 3, pp. 439–45

North East of Scotland Child Protection Committee (2003) *Child Review Report into the Life and Death of Carla Nicole Bone 07-04-01–13-05-02*

O'Brien, S., Hammond, H. and McKinnon, M. (2003) *Report of the Caleb Ness Inquiry*, Edinburgh: Edinburgh and Lothian Child Protection Committee

O'Donnell, M., Scott, D. and Stanley, F. (2008) 'Child abuse and neglect – is it time for a public health approach?', *Australian and New Zealand Journal of Public Health*, Vol. 32, No. 4, pp. 325–30

Office for National Statistics (2007) Mortality statistics: childhood, infant and perinatal, England and Wales, www.statistics.gov.uk

Ofsted (2008a) *Learning Lessons, Taking Action: Ofsted's Evaluation of Serious Case Reviews 1 April 2007 to 31 March 2008*, London: Ofsted

Ofsted (2008b) *Safeguarding Children. The Third Joint Chief Inspectors' Report on Arrangements to Protect Children*, London: Ofsted

Onwuachi-Saunders, C., Forjuoh, S. N., West, P. and Brooks, C. (1999) 'Child death reviews: a gold mine for injury prevention and control', *Injury Prevention*, Vol. 5, No. 4, pp. 276–9

Owen, H. (2009) 'Doing Serious Case Reviews well: politics, academia, risk management and staff care', in Hughes, L. and Owen, H. (2009) *Good Practice in Safeguarding Children*, London: Jessica Kingsley

Owers, M., Brandon, M. and Black, J. (1999) *Learning How to Make Children Safer: An Analysis of Serious Child Abuse Cases in Wales*, University of East Anglia/Welsh Office

Parton, N. (1996) 'Social work, risk and the blaming system', in Parton, N. (ed.) (1996) *Social Theory, Social Change and Social Work*, London: Routledge

Parton, N. (2004) 'From Maria Colwell to Victoria Climbie: reflections on public inquiries into child abuse a generation apart', *Child Abuse Review*, Vol. 13, No. 2, pp. 80–94

Pearson, G. A. (ed.) (2008) *Why Children Die: A Pilot Study 2006, England (South West, North East and West Midlands), Wales and Northern Ireland*, London, CEMACH

Pearson, R. (2009) 'Working with unco-operative or hostile families', in Hughes, L. and Owen, H. (2009) *Good Practice in Safeguarding Children*, London: Jessica Kingsley

Peckover, S. (2009) 'Domestic abuse and safeguarding children', in Hughes, L. and Owen, H. (2009) *Good Practice in Safeguarding Children*, London: Jessica Kinsgley

Pringle, K. (1993) 'Child sexual abuse perpetrated by welfare personnel and the problem of men', *Critical Social Policy*, Vol. 36, 4–19

Pritchard, C. and Sharples, A. (2008) '"Violent" deaths of children in England and Wales and the major developed countries 1974–2002: possible evidence of improving child protection?', *Child Abuse Review*, Vol. 17, No. 5, pp. 297–312

Radford, L. and Hester, M. (2006) *Mothering through Domestic Violence*, London: Jessica Kingsley

RCPATH and RCPCH (2004) *Sudden Unexpected Death in Infancy: a Multi-agency Protocol for Care and Investigation*, London: Royal College of Pathologists/Royal College of Paediatrics and Child Health

Reder, P and Duncan, S. (1996) 'Reflections on child abuse inquiries', in Peay, J. (ed.) (1996) *Inquiries after Homicide*, London: Duckworth

Reder, P. and Duncan, S. (1999) *Lost Innocents: A Follow up Study of Fatal Child Abuse*, London: Routledge

Reder, P. and Duncan S. (2004) 'From Colwell to Climbie: inquiring into fatal child abuse', in Stanley, N. and Manthorpe, J. (eds) (2004) *The Age of the Inquiry: Learning and Blaming in Health and Social Care*, London: Routledge

Reder, P., Duncan, S. and Gray, M. (1993) *Beyond Blame: Child Abuse Tragedies Revisited*, London: Brunner-Routledge

Reder, P., McClure, M. and Jolley, A. (eds) (2000) *Family Matters: Interfaces between Child and Adult Mental Health*, London: Routledge

Rimsza, M. E., Schackner, R. A., Bowen, K. A. and Marshall, W. (2002) 'Can child deaths be prevented? The Arizona Child Fatality Review Program experience', *Pediatrics*, Vol. 110, e11

Rose, W. and Barnes, J. (2008) *Improving Safeguarding Practice: Study of Serious Case Reviews 2001–2003*, London: Department for Children, Schools and Families

Rustin, M. (2005) 'Conceptual analysis of critical moments in Victoria Climbie's life', *Child and Family Social Work*, Vol. 10, pp. 11–19

Sanders, R., Colton, M. and Roberts, S. (1999) 'Child abuse fatalities and cases of extreme concern: lessons from reviews', *Child Abuse and Neglect*, Vol. 23, No. 3, pp. 257–68

Schnitzer, P. and Ewigman, B. (2005) 'Child deaths resulting from inflicted injuries: household risk factors and perpetrator characteristics', *Pediatrics*, Vol. 116, pp. 687–93

Scottish Education Department, Social Work Services Group (1975) *Report of the Committee into the Consideration Given and Steps Taken towards Securing the Welfare of Richard Clark by Perth Town Council and other Bodies or Persons Concerned*, Edinburgh: HMSO

Scottish Executive (2002) *'It's Everyone's Job to Make Sure I'm Alright': Report of the Child Protection Audit and Review*, Edinburgh: Astron

Scottish Executive (2006) *Changing Lives: Report of the 21st Century Social Work Review*, Edinburgh: Astron

Scottish Executive (2007) 'Protecting children and young people: interim guidance for Child Protection Committees for conducting a Significant Case Review' (online). Available from URL: www.scotland.gov.uk/Publications/2007/03/30114400/0 (accessed 3 August 2009)

Secretary of State for Social Services (1988) *Report of the Inquiry into Child Abuse in Cleveland 1987*, London: HMSO

Sen, R., Kendrick, A., Milligan, I. and Hawthorn, M. (2007) 'Historical abuse in residential child care in Scotland 1950–1995: a literature review', in Shaw, T. (2007) *Historical Abuse Systemic Review*, Edinburgh: Scottish Government

Sidebotham, P. (2001) *Child Abuse in the Pre-school Population: An Ecological Analysis of Risk and Protective Factors*, The Research Findings Register, Summary No. 638

Sidebotham, P. J. and Fleming, P. (2007) (eds) *Unexpected Death in Childhood*, Chichester: Wiley

Sidebotham, P., Fox, J., Horwath, J., Powell, C. and Perwez, S. (2008) *Preventing Childhood Deaths: an Observational Study of Child Death Overview Panels in England*, London: Department for Children, Schools and Families

Sinclair, R. and Bullock, R. (2002) *Learning from Past Experience: A Review of Serious Case Reviews*, London: Department of Health

Skinner, A. (1992) *Another Kind of Home: A Review of Residential Child Care*, Edinburgh: The Scottish Office

Social Services Inspectorate (1994) *Evaluating Child Protection Services: Child Protection Inspections 1993/4; Overview Report of 8 Inspections*

Social Work Inspection Agency (SWIA) (2005) *An Inspection into the Care and Protection of Children in Eilean Siar*, Edinburgh: Scottish Executive

Social Work Inspection Agency (SWIA)/HM Inspectorate of Constabulary (HMIC) (2005) *Review of the Management Arrangements of Colyn Evans by Fife Constabulary and Fife Council*, Edinburgh: Scottish Executive

Stafford, A. and Vincent, S. (eds) (2008) *Safeguarding and Protecting Children and Young People*, Edinburgh: Dunedin

Staffordshire County Council (1991) *The Pindown Experience and the Protection of Children*, Staffordshire County Council

Stanley, N. and Manthorpe, J. (eds) (2004) *The Age of the Inquiry: Learning and Blaming in Health and Social Care*, London: Routledge

Utting, W. (1991) *Children in the Public Care: A Review of Residential Child Care*, London: HMSO

Ward Platt, M. P. (2007) 'Child death reviews: progress in the north of England', *Exchange*, Vol. 4, Summer

Warner, N. (1992) *Choosing with Care: The Report of the Committee of Inquiry into the Selection, Development and Management of Staff in Children's Homes*, London: HMSO

Waterhouse, R. (2000) *Lost in Care: Report of the Tribunal of Inquiry into the Abuse of Children in Care in the Former County Council areas of Gwynedd and Clwyd since 1974*, London: The Stationery Office

Webster, R., Schnitzer, P., Jenny, C., Ewigman, B. and Alario, A. (2003) 'Child death review: the state of the nation', *American Journal of Preventative Medicine*, Vol. 25, pp. 58–64

Welsh Assembly Government (2006) *Safeguarding Children: Working Together under the Children Act 2004*

Welsh Assembly Government (2008) 'Local Safeguarding Children Boards, Wales: Review of Regulations and Guidance' (online). Available from URL: http://wales.gov.uk/topics/childrenyoungpeople/publications/localsafeguarding/?lang=en

Wilczynski, A. (1995) 'Risk factors for parental child homicide', *Current Issues in Criminal Justice*, Vol. 7, No. 2, pp. 193–222

Index